Contents

The War Against Grammar

David Mulroy

New Perspectives in Rhetoric and Composition

CHARLES I. SCHUSTER, SERIES EDITOR

Boynton/Cook Publishers, Inc.
HEINEMANN
Portsmouth, NH

Boynton/Cook Publishers, Inc.
A subsidiary of Reed Elsevier Inc.
361 Hanover Street
Portsmouth, NH 03801-3912
www.boyntoncook.com

Offices and agents throughout the world

Library of Congress Cataloging-in-Publication Data
Mulroy, David D., 1943–
The war against grammar / David Mulroy.
    p. cm.—(CrossCurrents)
    Includes bibliographical references and index.
    ISBN 0-86709-551-2
    1. Language and languages—Study and teaching. 2. Grammar, Comparative and general—Study and teaching (Higher). 3. Teachers—Training of. I. Title.
    II. Series: CrossCurrents (Portsmouth, N.H.).

P53.85.M85 2003
418'.0071'1—dc21

                                                                          2003007515

Editor: Charles I. Schuster
Production service: The GTS Companies/York, PA Campus
Production coordinator: Elizabeth Valway
Cover design: Joni Doherty
Manufacturing: Steve Bernier

Printed in the United States of America on acid-free paper
07 06 05 04   DA   2 3 4 5

The War Against Grammar

Erasmus

Also in the CrossCurrents series

Foreword

Let me begin with a confession: I teach grammar. Not some enlightened form of grammatical analysis based on post-Chomskyian analytics—no, I am talking about good, old-fashioned traditional grammatical structure: nouns and verbs, subjects and predicates, transitives and intransitives, direct and indirect objects, phrases and clauses. Along the way, I include discussions and exercises on adjectives and adverbs along with adjectival and adverbial phrases and clauses, infinitives, gerunds, prepositions, participles, verb tense and mood, the forms of *to be*, the seven coordinate conjunctions, predicate nominatives, restrictive and nonrestrictive relative clauses, the subjunctive, and—that greatest bugbear of all—usage and correctness, with a focus on the niceties of expression (between–among, it–its, dangling participles, comma splices, split infinitives, the use of fragments). It is true that I integrate these discussions within an overall emphasis on style, the recasting of language, sentence combining, Christensen's generative grammar, Weathers and Winchester's Grammar B, rhetoric as argument and persuasion. But there's no denying it: I believe students, especially English majors, need a grammatical understanding of how language works. Thus, I approached David Mulroy's manuscript with sympathy even before turning to the first page. And I read it through with pleasure, impressed by his knowledge of the classics, his grasp of rhetorical history related to grammar, and his fierce devotion to his subject.

The War Against Grammar enters into a decades (centuries?)–long debate about the use and misuse of grammar in the English classroom. It does so from an unusual perspective: Mulroy is not a teacher of writing nor an English teacher. He is a classicist devoted to teaching and translating Greek and Latin; his latest book is a translation of the poems of Catullus along with a commentary, and before we typecast him as a stuffy out-of-touch academic, it is worth noting that the University of Wisconsin Press, which published his *The Complete Poetry of Catullus*, notes that Mulroy "has performed his translations of Catullus' poems at poetry slams in Milwaukee bars to enthusiastic response." Although Mulroy is a colleague of mine at the University of Wisconsin-Milwaukee, I've not yet witnessed these slams, but it seems to me that the same strongly performative nature is at work on every page of this book.

For Mulroy, grammar is fundamental because it is constitutive to meaning. Largely uninterested in impressionistic responses and interpretive debates about the meanings of texts, Mulroy argues that an education centered on language mastery should emphasize literalized understanding of what a text means and how that meaning is created through grammatical structure. "The meaning of a sentence is created in part by the rules of grammar," Mulroy states early on. "Of these, the most important apply not to individual words but to whole classes of them—i.e., the parts of speech." One can hear in these words the fundamental assumptions of a foreign language educator devoted to literary translation: what students need is a concrete understanding of the meaning of the text, an understanding that often requires that one parse sentences and paragraphs. "Explication de texte," one of my graduate professors used to say repeatedly during class, "explication de texte." How can you engage in interpretation, she'd admonish, unless you understand literally what the words on the page mean?

Mulroy illustrates this point by quoting his students' paraphrases of the first sentence of the Declaration of Independence. Admittedly, the syntax is difficult and the implied references challenging, but for Mulroy the inability of most college students to make basic sense of these words represents "a higher illiteracy," one that results from our students' lacking the necessary tools to analyze "the precise interpretation of the meaning of complex statements." To paraphrase in this fashion is to engage in a form of imitation, the kind of strategy that Quintilian recommends and that I have found useful at all levels of teaching composition.

Much of Mulroy's book is devoted to an historical analysis of grammar: its origins, its importance during Greek and Roman times, the vagaries of its fortune in Europe and America, the misreadings of it by well-intentioned (or perhaps not-so-well-intentioned) researchers and NCTE/CCCC/WPA stalwarts who, in Mulroy's view, misread key texts or misapply fundamental concepts. He offers a reading that is at once grounded in historical understanding and radical in its views about language—radical because it calls for a sharp turn back toward a fundamental approach to language arts. At a time when so much of our professional literature is calling for us to expand our range of what is acceptable in formal and academic discourse, Mulroy is asking that we continue to uphold "standard English" as a desired outcome for our students...and ourselves. "Conscious knowledge of the nature of the sentence, the parts of speech, the conjugation of verbs, and the meanings of individual words enhances our ability to use and comprehend language pervasively," he states.

From my perspective, Mulroy's radical call for us to teach the eight parts of speech, sentence diagramming, and the literal understanding of works of complex prose bears only an indirect relation to the teaching of writing at the college level. Mulroy is not asking that we teach grammar in English 101; on the contrary, Mulroy's own attempts to teach grammar to college students for the most part failed miserably and thus would almost certainly be unproductive. Instead, Mulroy is arguing that the teaching of traditional grammatical analysis in certain parts of the curriculum will produce two valuable benefits.

First, future English/language arts teachers will be better prepared if we can impart to them at least some basic grammatical knowledge, both for their own education and so that they can better educate their students. As most teachers and linguists would agree, the optimal time to teach grammatical analysis is somewhere between grades 4 and 10. Unfortunately, few English or language arts teachers now have the necessary educational background to teach grammar or to integrate it within their lesson plans. There is only one way for them to obtain this knowledge: it has to be taught explicitly in the college curriculum. English departments are arguably the best place for such courses to be offered; many of us in composition, at least, have acquired an understanding of grammar, stylistics, linguistics, and the history of language—and can apply it meaningfully within a writing curriculum. Who better than us to teach future teachers about useful and creative ways to analyze language?

Certainly, it is hard to argue that English/language arts teachers do not need to have a sound understanding of traditional grammatical principles, especially as those principles apply to developing stylistic and rhetorical fluency, engaging in syntactic analysis, and moving between and among various dialects and languages. Certainly, it can only be helpful to such teachers to be able to explain to students, in meaningful grammatical terms, why some sentences work better than others and why a specific language construction makes sense while another leads to unintentional confusion and lack of clarity. When I think about how I could build on such a foundation at the college level, at least in some of my more advanced courses on style and rhetoric, I find myself planning a more sophisticated curriculum than is now possible.

Second, Mulroy traces the dramatic decline in foreign language education that is in evidence throughout the country at least in part to a decline in the teaching of grammar. Enrollments are down in virtually all languages but Spanish; in some universities, foreign language education is being downsized or altogether abandoned. Of course, there are multiple causes for this decline, but Mulroy is convinced—and I agree with him here—that students are struggling when it comes to learning foreign languages because they lack the grammatical knowledge to make connections between English and similar structures in French or German, Spanish or Russian, Latin or Greek. One of the fundamental ways we learn foreign language within an educational setting is to apply the grammatical principles of our native language to the structures of the target language. I can understand how the genitive works in Latin or German because I have some sense of how genitive constructions work in English; conversely, I can create better sentences as a writer in English as a result of studying absolute constructions in Latin. Certainly, an understanding of grammar might also provide a degree of confidence to students, thus encouraging them to enroll in foreign language courses.

But I have said enough, especially since David Mulroy articulates his perspective so much better than I do. He has written a provocative, thoughtful, informative book—one that challenges us to come to terms, once more, with the uses and abuses of grammatical instruction. I hope you find the book as stimulating as I do, both for its mastery of the subject and its passionate advocacy for a return to language education based on principles and practices rooted in Grammar, that most important of the original seven liberal arts.

CHARLES I. SCHUSTER

Preface

I have taught "Classics"—i.e., ancient Greek and Roman language, literature, and history—at the University of Wisconsin-Milwaukee since 1973. During these years, I have noticed a decline in the verbal abilities of my students. It is embodied in the difficulties that they have in reading comprehension and English composition as well as in the fact that few are capable of studying a foreign language successfully. The cause of this decline has never seemed mysterious to me. My students generally lack an understanding of basic grammatical concepts. Put most simply, they cannot classify words by part of speech. Most can identify prototypical examples of nouns, adjectives, verbs, and adverbs, but beyond that they are in the dark. Few know that *am* is a verb, for example. It is rare to encounter a student who can define participles.

Until 1996, I did not suspect that anyone questioned the value of knowing the parts of speech. They provide the basic taxonomy of words. The first step in mastering any field is gaining an overview of its structure, which requires classification of its elements. For example, I was a baseball fan as a youngster and effortlessly learned by heart the starting lineups (excluding pitchers) of all the teams in the American league. In those days, teams were fewer in number and positions more stable, but I could not have memorized a list of sixty-four names without the matrix provided by the different defensive positions. This is merely a matter of common sense. To get a handle on the data in the field, the first thing you must do is to sort them out according to a reasonable system of classification.

The meaning of a sentence is created in part by the rules of grammar. Of these, the most important apply not to individual words but to whole classes of them—i.e., the parts of speech. For example, a declarative sentence is a proposition about a subject, which is represented by a noun or a pronoun. The sense of the proposition is contained in the predicate, which begins with a finite verb—not a participle, and so on. Though we understand the sense of most utterances intuitively, the only reliable way to interpret obscure ones is through grammatical analysis, and that presupposes knowing the parts of speech. Moreover, if we wish to improve the ways in which we express ourselves either in writing or in speaking, we must think about grammatical patterns. For example, it is good advice to use the passive voice sparingly, but to benefit from that rule we have to understand what is meant by *passive voice*—i.e., it consists of a form of the verb *be* plus a past participle. Finally, grammar is the foundation of the study of foreign language. The reason that contemporary American students struggle with infinitives, participles, articles, demonstratives, and direct and indirect objects in foreign language classes is that they know very little about these entities in English.

In 1996, Wisconsin's Department of Public Instruction was drafting a new set of academic standards for the state's public schools and invited suggestions from the general public. At a public hearing, I recommended that high school seniors be required to identify the eight parts of speech in a selection of normal prose, thinking that such a modest and reasonable suggestion would be immediately embraced by all concerned. I followed this recommendation with a letter to the editor of the *Milwaukee Journal*. To my surprise, I found myself embroiled in a controversy. While the educational experts in charge of drafting the standards expressed no interest in adopting my suggestion, it was endorsed by a parents' group advocating educational reforms. This led to my brief involvement in the drafting of Wisconsin's Academic Standards. During this process, I discovered that my suggestion ran directly counter to conventional wisdom among experts in K–12 education. A consultant working for the Department of Public Instruction kindly showed me a printout from the Internet entitled "Facts on the teaching of grammar." This was a web page produced by the National Council of Teachers of English (NCTE), the nation's leading professional group of English teachers, the equivalent of the American Medical Association or the American Bar Association. According to this website, "decades of research" had shown that instruction in "formal grammar" did not accomplish any positive goals and was actually harmful because it took time away from more profitable activities.[1]

The use of the term "formal grammar" in NCTE statements confused me for some time. Grammar is all formal: it consists entirely of rules and definitions. I eventually perceived that what the NCTE actually opposes is *formal instruction* in grammar—i.e., asking students to memorize definitions, classify words by part of speech, parse verbs, and so forth. The council does not oppose the incidental use of grammatical terms and explanations by teachers. A teacher might mention, for example, that "some people call this kind of word a participle," but asking a student to say what a participle *is* or even to point to one would be viewed as counterproductive.

That *the* professional association of English teachers should issue a warning *against* the rigorous teaching of English grammar struck me as both ironic and symptomatic of a serious problem. I was ineluctably drawn away from my own academic specialty, translating ancient Greek and Latin poetry, into the research that has come to fruition in these pages. My purpose is to persuade the reader that formal instruction in grammar ought to be emphasized in K–12 education, especially in the middle grades, fourth through sixth. It is particularly important that students be able to classify words according to the parts of speech. This change is long overdue, and I had hoped that it would become part of American academic reform, as is currently the situation in England. Perhaps this book will be a step in that direction.

Note

1. The message reproduced on the web page represents the NCTE's official position. I later obtained a copy of memo from Millie Davis, director of Affiliate and Member Services, addressed to "Those Requesting Information on Grammar Instruction" and dated "Spring, 2001." The text of the memo reads: "Enclosed please find NCTE's position on the teaching of grammar within the context of English language arts instruction along with several suggested resources. If you have further questions, please feel free to consult the NCTE Web site at [*www.ncte.org*] or call 800-369-6283, ext. 3634." A page of quotations critical of instruction in grammar follows. Its title is "Slate Starter Sheet—Fact Sheet Series: #3 On the Teaching of Grammar." At the end of the page, a box advertising subscriptions to its newsletter reads in part: "Are you a member of SLATE? SLATE is NCTE's intellectual freedom network, focusing on numerous education issues and working intensively in combating censorship."

Acknowledgments

I have been the recipient of much helpful encouragement and advice while working on this book. I am particularly indebted in this regard to Leah Vukmir, founder of PRESS (Parents Raising Educational Standards in Schools), and Mary Campbell Gallagher, a New York educator and author, who frequently sends me emails with the subject line: "Your Marvelous Book." I was able to devote several summer months exclusively to work on the book because of generous grants from the Smith Richardson Foundation and the Windway Foundation. That most distinguished champion of grammar, Martha Kolln, read my manuscript and gave me a great deal of encouragement and constructive advice, despite our disagreement on several issues. The sympathetic interest of my friend, colleague, and now editor Chuck Schuster brought the project to fruition more quickly than I had thought possible.

I made more than my usual number of trips outside of the ivory tower to do research in the field, as it were, and met many wonderful individuals. Most outstanding as a group were the grade school students at the Calvert School, the Independence School, the Brookfield Academy, Elm Grove Lutheran, and elsewhere who were turned on intellectually by the formal study of traditional grammar. Of these, a boy from the Brookfield Academy was the most memorable, though I never learned his name. He was the first out of the gate with an example of "a linking sentence having a transitive gerund as its subject"—viz., "Spewing chunks is unpleasant." I humbly dedicate this little book to him.

Chapter One

America the Grammarless

A Point Generally Conceded

Q. How well was the purpose of this course fulfilled?
A. Thier [*sic*] was no purpose.
(From a student's negative evaluation of the author's freshman seminar on traditional grammar)

Hardly anything one says about the state of American education will go uncontested for long. An exception to this rule, however, is the assertion that students who have come of age in our nation since the sixties have very little grasp of grammar. The ignorance of the Boomers' babies in this regard is a familiar fact of life, like the popularity of television and fast food, and is alluded to whenever language arts education is discussed. Here is a typical reference in passing by author David Foster Wallace, writing in *Harper's Magazine:*[1]

> I teach college English part-time—mostly Lit, not Comp. But I am also so pathologically anal about usage that every semester the same thing happens: The minute I have read my students' first set of papers, we immediately abandon the regular Lit syllabus and have a three-week Emergency Remedial Usage Unit, during which my demeanor is basically that of somebody teaching HIV prevention to intravenous-drug users. When it emerges (as it does, every time) that *95 percent of these intelligent upscale college students have never been taught, e.g., what a clause is* [emphasis added] or why a misplaced *only* can make a sentence confusing, I all but pound my head on the blackboard; I exhort them to sue their hometown school boards.

Wallace's essay concerns proper usage rather than its conceptual underpinnings. As this excerpt shows, he adopts a light-hearted attitude toward people like himself who feel that usage is important. What

1

strikes me, however, is his statement in passing that few college students know what a clause is. This has been borne out by my own experience and is consistent with the things generally said about college English classes. Am I alone in finding such ignorance remarkable? It is difficult to think of a concept more fundamental to understanding language than that of a clause. Most of Wallace's students have had more than twelve years of English classes and have performed relatively well in them. If twelve years of chemistry classes produced students who could only stare blankly when asked to describe *molecules,* would people then agree that the curriculum needed to be refocused?

The students are not to blame. As we will see, the problem started with teachers deciding not to teach grammar. Several decades later, many teachers could not teach grammar if they chose to because they themselves have never had any formal instruction in the subject.

A litmus test for grammatical understanding is the *passive voice.* Teachers of English composition normally avoid using grammatical terminology, but they usually mention the passive voice. This is because George Orwell recommended avoidance of the passive voice as a general rule in his famous essay, "Politics and the English Language." Perhaps because it is thus associated with politics, the rule has become very popular—even though the majority of students who hear about it and many of the teachers who promulgate it are unaware of what the passive voice is. Here is a typical anecdote from a professor of English, Herbert Stahlke, of Ball State University:

> We can all come up with instances of grammatical ignorance in high places. My current favorite comes from an invitation I received to talk to a graduate composition methods classes about grammar and rhetoric. The instructor gave me a couple of xeroxes from articles dealing with how teachers should mark student essays. In both examples, the model marker had flagged a sentence as passive, and therefore questionable, that was not passive, but clearly active with an experiencer subject. I asked the class what made the sentences "passive," and no one knew, but further discussion showed that no one knew what a passive sentence was either.[2]

I occasionally give diagnostic tests to my students to gauge the depth of the problem. I find that most can identify nouns, adjectives, verbs describing actions, and adverbs ending in -*ly*. Beyond that, their comprehension fades quickly. In a typical test taken by sixteen incoming freshmen, only four identified *rather* as an adverb in the phrase "rather charming"; only three knew that *am* was a verb in the sentence, "Am I really your son?" Only three could spot a verb in the passive voice. There was only one correct example each of a noun used as the object of a preposition, of a verb in a perfect tense, and of an infinitive.[3]

Such results are more significant than low scores on trivia tests. Grammatical terms are part of an orderly set of concepts that describe the organizational features of all intelligible speech and writing. Ignorance of the part of speech of *am* is particularly telling. The verb *be* in its various forms is of fundamental importance in understanding English grammar. For example, the rule for making the passive voice is that you combine the appropriate form of *be* with the past participle of the verb in question. But this rule means nothing to students who do not know that *am, is, are, was, were,* and *been* are forms of *be.* When I began teaching, I never imagined that I would ever encounter a college student who did not understand such an elementary fact. It was a watershed event in my career when I realized that few of my students knew what I meant by "the verb *to be.*" They thought I was referring to a word that was destined to become a verb.

It is hard to give any kind of language instruction to students who lack the conceptual framework provided by the terms of basic grammar. Moreover, the deficit is difficult to remedy when students reach the college level. Though grammatical concepts seem simple and obvious to people who understand them, they are very difficult for older students to master for the first time. Perhaps, the ability to grasp them is one of those aptitudes that atrophy after puberty. The general phenomenon of diminishing aptitude for language learning has been established by modern researchers.[4] That grammar is most easily learned by the young was a familiar truth during the English Renaissance. It is alluded to in an elegant preface to a 1673 edition of Lily's *Grammar*, a famous textbook discussed below. Grammar, writes the anonymous author,

> as she is a severe mistress, is also a coy one and hardly admits of any courtship but of the youthful votary. There are indeed many who by great industry have redeemed the want of early institution but in the performances of such there still appears somewhat of stiffness and force and what has more in it of art than nature.

This is a hard truth that I have learned from experience. On three separate occasions, I have devoted entire semesters to trying to teach the parts of speech, sentence diagramming, and the conjugation of English verbs to groups of college freshmen, for whom my course was a freely chosen elective. In other words, at some point, these students *wanted* to study grammar. At the end, the only students who had any facility in identifying the parts of speech were the few who entered the course already understanding them fairly well. The others displayed an inability to master the subject that had all the appearances of a hostile determination not to. It was like trying to teach table manners to a motorcycle gang.

There has probably never been a time when some teachers did not complain about the ignorance of "modern students" in some field. Skeptical readers will assume that I have fallen prey to the common illusion that in the good old days students were smarter and worked harder than they are or do today. Indeed, older people are often misled in this way. On the other hand, in addition to the myth of the golden age, there is an equally strong current that drags others off in the opposite direction. This was identified by Daniel Patrick Moynihan in his well-known essay, "Defining Deviancy Down." As the title implies, he gives examples of a widespread tendency to deny that intransigent problems exist by redefining *normalcy*. He points out, for example, that the annual number of traffic fatalities—viz., "somewhat less than 50,000"—now accepted as normal is close to the level that was considered a major public health problem in the sixties. The "recentering" of Scholastic Aptitude Test (SAT) scores suggests that something similar has been occurring in education. In any event, the impulse to "solve" problems by denying their existence is as strong as the impulse to romanticize past practice. Only by examining the particulars of a given case can one decide which impulse is obscuring the truth.

English Teachers to Their Students: "Stop Studying Grammar!"

The difficulty of generalizing about America's classrooms is increased by their number and their diversity. Local school boards enjoy great freedom in setting policies, and they normally grant individual teachers a good deal of latitude. In a country as large and diverse as the United States, anecdotal evidence can be collected in support of virtually any proposition. Still, the fact that the leadership of the largest and most influential association of English teachers has been urging its members for decades to pay less attention to formal instruction in grammar lends credence to the widespread impression that our students' understanding of that subject is at an all-time low.

The National Council of Teachers of English (NCTE) was founded in 1911, now claims 80,000 members, and publishes thirteen separate journals and frequent special reports. Its members are English teachers in K–12 schools, English composition teachers in colleges and universities, and faculty members specializing in the language arts in schools of education. Over the years, NCTE publications have often provided a platform for teachers opposed to emphasizing grammar. Their anti-grammar stance is especially associated with the name of

Charles Fries, a linguist from the University of Michigan. Fries first came to notice in 1925 with the publication by the Modern Language Association of his doctoral dissertation on the use of *shall* and *will*[5] and was a prominent member of the NCTE for many years. He advocated the use of scientific methods by linguists. This meant that linguists needed to part company from traditional grammarians in two ways: First, they should refrain from telling people how they ought to express themselves and concentrate instead on describing the facts of language. Second, their definitions and rules should not require any intuitive judgments but should be based solely on empirical observations.

In urging these restrictions, Fries played a role in laying the foundation of modern linguistics, but his influence was not entirely positive. One of the major themes of this book is that there is no necessary conflict between scientific linguistics and traditional grammar. They are complementary endeavors, one theoretical and the other practical. Unfortunately, Fries was inclined to see their relationship differently. His most influential work, *The Structure of English* (1952), was cited as recently as 1991 in the NCTE handbook of research as the "strongest and most typical criticism" of traditional school grammar.[6] On the first page of *Structure*, Fries compares the new scientific attitude toward language to Harvey's work on the circulation of blood and traditional grammar to the practice of bleeding.[7] The clear implication was that traditional grammar ought to be discouraged—outlawed, if possible. The result of Fries's work, therefore, was a mixed legacy. On the positive side, he was one of the founding fathers of twentieth-century linguistics, but negatively his authority lent weight to the false belief that modern linguists had discredited traditional grammar.

As the image of bleeding suggests, academics opposed to formal instruction in grammar see themselves as enlightened progressives trying to win over a public that is blindly devoted to tradition. Everyday people assume that grammar is something that children should learn in "grammar school." Furthermore, in recent years, parents and politicians have attempted to mandate more attention to it among other subjects through new academic standards. This has contributed to the anti-grammarians' sense of righteous struggle. Hence, their arguments are sometimes couched in rhetoric reminiscent of political campaigns for civil rights or against censorship. In fact, the NCTE group that disseminates its critique of formal instruction in grammar describes itself as an "intellectual freedom network" whose primary responsibility is opposing censorship.[8]

The anti-grammarians' beliefs are summarized in two frequently quoted reports published by the NCTE. Strictly speaking, these address only the question of the effect of "formal grammar" on the writing abilities of students. Since English teachers are the people who teach grammar in grade school, if it is to be taught at all, and since English teachers view English composition as one of their highest priorities, the assertion that instruction in grammar hurts composition is, in practice, the same as saying that it should not be taught at all.

The first of the reports appeared in 1963 as *Research in Written Composition* by Richard Braddock, Richard Lloyd-Jones, and Lowell Schoer. The body of the report has been long forgotten, but its summary judgment on the value of instruction grammar has been frequently quoted in NCTE publications:

> In view of the widespread agreement of research studies based upon many types of students and teachers, the conclusion can be stated in strong and unqualified terms: the teaching of formal grammar has a negligible or, because it usually displaces some instruction and practice in composition, even a harmful effect on the improvement of writing.[9]

The reason for this statement's fame is its bold reversal of conventional wisdom: teaching grammar actually hurts writing.

This same negative attitude toward grammar was embodied in an official resolution adopted by the NCTE in 1985:

> Resolved, that the NCTE affirm the position that the use of isolated grammar and usage exercises not supported by theory and research is a deterrent to the improvement of students' speaking and writing and that, in order to improve both of these, class time at all levels must be devoted to opportunities for meaningful listening, speaking, reading, and writing; and that NCTE urge the discontinuance of testing practices that encourage the teaching of grammar rather than the improvement of writing.[10]

Note that "the teaching of grammar" is excluded from, and even contrasted with, "English language arts."

The position was reaffirmed in 1991, when the NCTE issued an impressive volume entitled *Handbook of Research on Teaching the English Language Arts*. Its article on "Grammar and Usage" by George Hillocks, Jr., and Michael Smith states that the teaching of traditional grammar is not just useless but pernicious:

> School boards, administrators, and teachers who impose the systematic study of traditional school grammar on their students over lengthy periods of time in the name of teaching writing do them a gross disservice which should not be tolerated by anyone concerned with the effective teaching of good writing.[11]

The campaign to de-emphasize grammar was consistent with and reinforced by approaches to instruction in writing that became fashionable in the sixties. Typical of the period is an influential textbook,

Writing With Power, by Peter Elbow. According to Elbow, attention to grammar is not just harmful to writing; it is also dangerous to one's mental health:

> Learning grammar is a formidable task that takes crucial energy away from working on your writing, and worse yet, the process of learning grammar interferes with writing; it heightens your preoccupation with mistakes as you write out each word and phrase, and makes it almost impossible to achieve that undistracted attention to your thoughts and experiences as you write that is so crucial for strong writing (and sanity). For most people, nothing helps their writing so much as learning to ignore grammar.[12]

Not all books on language arts pedagogy are entirely negative. A more moderate attitude was adopted by Constance Weaver, whose book *Teaching Grammar in Context* enjoys great prestige in NCTE circles. As her title implies, Weaver takes advantage of the loophole provided by NCTE statements against teaching grammar *in isolation*. As interpreted by her, however, teaching a subject in context comes very close to not teaching it at all:

> Introduce only a minimum of terminology, much of which can be learned sufficiently just through incidental exposure—for example, as we discuss selected words and structures in the context of literature and writing. For many grammatical terms, receptive competence is all that's needed: that is, students need to understand what the teacher is referring to, but they do not always need enough command of the terms to use such terms themselves.[13]

"Receptive competence" looks like jargon used to promote an idea that is implausible when expressed in plain words. The fact that people cannot use certain terms themselves is a clear sign that they do not fully understand them. If so, they are quite likely to misinterpret what other people mean by them. Teachers who aim at "receptive competence" are disregarding a pedagogical principle that is almost too obvious to state—viz., explanations work best when the terms employed are fully understood by all involved.

To be fair, Weaver's approach makes sense as a way of teaching writing to college students who did not learn about grammar in grade school. My own travails in the freshman seminar mentioned earlier showed me how hard it is to teach elementary grammar to older students. There is, therefore, a need for textbooks on English composition designed for the grammatically challenged. Viewed as such, the efforts of authors like Elbow and Weaver are to be applauded. The problem is that such authors are naturally inclined to make a virtue of necessity, presenting their ungrammatical approaches to writing instruction as the ideal method rather than a concession to harsh reality.

This exacerbates the underlying problem by sending the message to grade school teachers that there is no need for their students to learn grammar.

The Internet has made it easy to sample the opinions of professional groups, not least English teachers. Among the lists on which they make their feelings known is a very active one for writing program administrators. Participants are chiefly university and college faculty members who run English composition programs and hence exercise great influence over the way English is taught. The subject of grammar frequently arises. A glance at the contributions makes is obvious that the NCTE views of grammar enjoy unquestioned supremacy among language arts professionals. The NCTE's statement that teaching "formal" grammar does not improve writing but could have detrimental effects is constantly repeated.[14]

Although the NCTE's opposition to grammar dominates professional opinion, it has not gone entirely unchallenged. In 1983, Ed Vavra, a literature and language arts specialist at Shenandoah College in Winchester, Virginia (but now at the Pennsylvania College of Technology), began publishing a newsletter, *Syntax in the Schools,* dedicated to restoring interest in professional circles in grammar instruction. He circulated it at his own expense to potentially sympathetic colleagues. By the summer of 1990, he had attracted enough interest and support to hold a conference at Shenandoah, which was attended by twenty-seven individuals. The keynote address was given by Martha Kolln, a professor of English at Pennsylvania State University and the author of a highly regarded textbook on English grammar, then in its third edition.[15] The event marked the birth of the Association for the Teaching of English Grammar. Three years later, the association was recognized by the NCTE as an official interest group and was renamed the Assembly for the Teaching of English Grammar, or ATEG. The ATEG continues in operation and now claims several hundred members. I attended its annual conference in Minnesota in July of 2000. Kolln was retiring as president and gave an eloquent and informative speech[16] recounting the history of the organization and the progress that it had made in restoring interest and respectability to the subject of grammar. Yet to a relative outsider, the circumstances were surrealistic. On the one hand, there was a huge, well-financed association of English teachers, the NCTE, crusading *against* English grammar. Later that year, it would hold its annual meeting in my hometown, Milwaukee. It would be attended by several thousand teachers, take up all available hotel space, and fill a large downtown exhibition center with exhibits. On the other hand, I found myself among twenty-some intellectual guerrillas, drawn from the entire nation—Pennsylvania, Missouri,

California—members of the despised, pro-grammar sect, not quite filling a single classroom in North Hennepin Community College, plotting ways to sneak terms like *participle* and *infinitive* into English classes. One conferee claimed that she had concealed the nature of the meeting from her supervisors because she feared reprisals.

That the prestige of teaching grammar has fallen so low lends credence to the impression that most contemporary college students do not understand it at all. Grammar is a demanding subject best learned at a young age when students are still forming their foundational linguistic habits. It must be taught slowly and systematically in a way that is suitable for the young. When grade school teachers understand basic concepts and teach them consistently, year after year, they endow their young students with a valuable foundation. In contrast, when many teachers have been convinced to ignore grammar and others do not understand it themselves, students will get sporadic instruction at best and some of it will be aimed only at "receptive competence." Under such circumstances, it is not surprising that most students arrive at college unable to define or recognize a clause.

Straws in the Wind 1: The ETS Study of Adult Literacy

There are indications that efficacy of language arts education in the United States declined markedly during the sixties and seventies, the same period in which opposition to instruction in formal grammar took on the character of official dogma in schools of education. A recent study by the Educational Testing Service (ETS) of adult literacy in the United States compared with the situation in other wealthy nations provides empirical indication of a problem in language arts education starting in the sixties. In this study, the reading abilities of various demographic cohorts in the United States were ranked against their counterparts in nineteen other high-income countries. As a whole, the performance of the United States was described by the ETS as being "mediocre"; in fact, the term applies only to the performance of Americans who entered school starting in the sixties. The report states that our oldest adults, fifty-six years and above, were the second most literate in comprehending connected prose, but—

> As we look to our younger cohorts, our advantage begins to diminish and then disappear. Our adults aged 46–55 and 36–45 also ranked in the top five among these high-income countries. Our youngest cohorts, however, those 26 to 35 and 16 to 25 years old, ranked only 11th and 14th respectively.[17]

The report concludes that our educational system is "clearly less productive [than those of other nations] in raising the literacy skills of students per dollar spent."

Straws in the Wind 2: SAT Scores

The clearest evidence of a problem in language arts instruction may lie in the well-known decline in the nation's SAT scores. Both verbal and quantitative scores began to sink in 1963, the year of the NCTE Braddock report discussed above. The average verbal score dropped over 50 points, from 478 in 1963 to the 420s in the seventies. The quantitative score fell from 502 to 466 in 1980. Subsequently, quantitative scores rebounded somewhat, but verbal scores stayed in the 420s. In 1996, The College Board "recentered" the SAT scores. The average verbal score for that year, 428, was reported as 505; the quantitative average was changed from 488 to 512.[18] In 2002, the recentered averages were 504 (verbal) and 516 (mathematics).

The SAT decline is not an indictment of every aspect of American education, but neither can it be dismissed as being entirely insignificant. The SATs are taken by only 30–40 percent of high school seniors. Those taking them are typically applying to elite colleges. Hence, their performance reflects the abilities of the nation's best students. Tests taken by broader segments of the student population—e.g., the Preliminary SATs—did not show similar declines.

It is sometimes thought that declining SAT scores reflected the fact that the pool of test takers had become less selective, but that was not the case. In fact, it was during the fifties that the pool of SAT takers became more democratic, increasing from 10 percent to nearly 40 with no significant change in aggregate scores. The decline in scores occurred in the sixties and seventies while the percentage of high school seniors taking the SAT was shrinking and probably becoming more selective.[19] The specific problem revealed was not that average students had less verbal ability but that fewer students had outstanding verbal ability. In 1972, the absolute number of students who scored over 600 on the verbal SAT was 116,585, 11.3% of the pool; in 1995, the last year before recentering, the number was 88,643, or 8.3%.[20] This problem is not as disturbing as a universal decline in verbal abilities would have been, but it is hardly an acceptable outcome. The American goal of ever-increasing access to higher education makes sense only if it means that the quality of higher education will at least remain constant while more and more students demonstrate the intellectual excellence necessary to benefit from it. According to SAT trends, that is what actually occurred during the fifties, but subsequent developments have produced markedly fewer college-bound students who could demonstrate outstanding verbal abilities. This creates downward pressure on the quality of college education, and it implies that some children *are* being left behind.

Straws in the Wind 3: Foreign Language Study

My children, seven and five, are Arabic/English bilinguals. They are in an Arabic medium school in Riyadh and receive eight hours of French instruction per week. I have noticed that formal grammar rules form an integral part of both Arabic and French (native and foreign language) instruction at their school and this appears to be the general practice in the Arab world. By the third grade children can already distinguish verbs from nouns, describe the function and use of adverbs and adjectives, and they know the technical vocabulary of grammar in both languages. I am teaching English grammar at one of Riyadh's universities. This task is made considerably easier by the students' unfailing knowledge of the core concepts of formal grammar and by their familiarity with the Arabic terminology used to describe it. . . . There are degrees of literacy. One of the cultural problems of the English speaking world is that it is cut away from its sources, from the common experience of the English speaking peoples spanning some seven centuries. That experience is contained, for the most part, in books, and most of those books are inaccessible to all but a fortunate few. The reason for that is obvious, at least to me.

—Omar Johnstone[21]

Another stark indicator of a problem is a decline in the percentage of students studying foreign language on the college level. In 1965, 16.5% of college credits were earned in foreign language courses. This figure fell to 7.8% in 1977 and has fluctuated between 7.3 and 8.2 since then. In 1998, the last year for which information is available, the figure stood at 7.9.[22] The authors of studies of trends in foreign language study are generally inclined to put an optimistic face on their statistics and emphasize short-term gains in the absolute numbers of students studying some languages. These gains, however, reflect the great increase in the numbers of students going to college. This total grew from 3,789,000 in 1960 to 14,590,000 in 1998.[23] During this growth spurt, enrollments in Spanish have remained constant as a percentage of the college population and have, therefore, recorded large increases in absolute numbers. Enrollments in the other most commonly taught languages declined sharply between 1965 and 1980 and have not rebounded. As in the case of the SATs, the problem seems to exist among a kind of elite: students who accept the challenge of foreign language courses, which are among the most difficult in the area of humanities. In terms of absolute numbers, there were 189,032 fewer American college students taking French in 1998 than in 1968 even though the college population had increased by more than seven million. Similarly, there were 127,253 fewer taking German and 16,905 fewer taking Russian. Between 1965 and 1998, there was a decline of 17,553 students studying classical languages, while the pool of college students increased by nine million.

Spanish has long enjoyed a reputation on American campuses as being the easiest of the foreign languages to learn as well as the most usable. Perhaps significant numbers of students fleeing more difficult languages take refuge in Spanish rather than dropping language study altogether. In any event, Spanish enrollments seem to have held their own. The decline in interest in other languages is not readily explicable. It has occurred in a period of highly publicized "globalization," when everyone is aware that knowledge of a second language brings many desirable opportunities with it. Moreover, language teachers have gone to great lengths to attract and keep students, transforming their profession in the process. Renate Schulz, a professor of German and Second-Language Acquisition at the University of Arizona, provides a good sense of the sea change that has occurred:

> In (the) good old days—which ended sometime around 1970—we had content-based instruction in the best sense of the word, the content being the language as such, that is, the phonetic and grammatical structures of the language we were teaching and how those compared with the sounds and patterns of English. We also touched on cultural patterns, particularly as they were reflected in the accepted literary canon of the time. We conjugated and declinated; we transformed singular forms to plurals and present tenses to the past. . . . Multiple intelligences, learning styles, and learning strategies were not yet topics under consideration.[24]

As Schulz intimates, emphasis on grammar in elementary language instruction is now passé. It has been replaced by various pedagogical innovations, especially the study of culture. The theory is that students will learn a language best by participation in cultural activities associated with it.[25] The theory is sometimes carried to foolish extremes. I eventually withdrew my son from public school in favor of home schooling. The last straw for me was a project in his *soi-disant* French class. He was required to prepare a dessert made out of mangoes and powdered sugar, supposedly a favorite in Francophone Africa. At this point, he had not learned anything about the conjugation of French verbs.

Whatever one makes of it, the emphasis on culture at the expense of grammar is far advanced in language classrooms. In fact, two professors writing in the Modern Language Association's journal for foreign language teachers speak of the transformation of foreign language departments into departments of foreign culture as nearly a fait accompli:

> The ongoing reinvention of foreign language and literature departments as cultural studies departments has placed renewed emphasis on the study of culture at the undergraduate level. In arguing for this institutional shift to cultural studies proponents cite a number of intellectual reasons, such as the need to interrogate the literary canon, as well as practical concerns, including the very survival of foreign language departments in the face of dwindling enrollments.[26]

In other words, foreign language teachers have generally responded to dwindling enrollments by emphasizing culture at the expense of grammar. This approach has yet to produce any dramatic improvement in enrollments. My hypothesis is that the problem lies not in the way that languages were or are taught in college, but in the fact that fewer students are given the foundation in grammar in grade school that is necessary to succeed in the later study of a foreign language, however it is taught. The fact that teachers have seen instruction in grammar as a problematic element in the curriculum lends credence to this hypothesis. Apparently, their students tend to lose interest when discussion turns to conjugating verbs; so, they break out the mangoes and powdered sugar.[27]

Straws in the Wind 4:
College Students' Writing Skills

What I saw horrified me: sentence fragments, gross spelling errors, punctuation misuse, jumbled thinking, and even sometimes no thinking at all. The pages were an alphabet soup, showcasing in black and white (and sometimes pink, purple and green) the huge disparity between the kind of writing produced by freshmen when I was in college and now. I remember putting that first pile of papers on the desk, placing my head in my hands and saying, "Oh, my God! What am I going to do? Where do I start?" I also wondered how it was that students who couldn't communicate in complete sentences, much less logical paragraphs, could be admitted to any university. Nevertheless, here they were.

—(Karen Heise on reading her first
student essays as a teacher of English
composition at the University of
Northern Colorado)[28]

Another indication of a problem in the language arts deserves mention, even though it is probably explained, at least in part, by the increasing numbers of students attending college. It is the prevalence of remedial courses in reading and English composition and of laments of the sort that I cite in the epigraph above. In a 1995 survey, 78 percent of colleges and universities offered at least one remedial reading, writing, or mathematics course, and 29 percent of first-time freshmen took at least one such course. Twenty-four percent took remedial mathematics, but the numbers in remedial reading and writing were substantial, 13 percent and 17 percent, respectively.[29] The researchers who compiled these statistics for the Institute for Higher Education Policy opined that remedial courses were probably underreported because a certain stigma was attached to them.

On my campus, a quarter of the 1999–2000 freshman class (767 of 3,066) placed in remedial English courses by their scores on a statewide English proficiency test.[30] According to teachers in these courses, the students involved are generally unable to write coherent paragraphs. Of these, ninety-seven placed in a pre-remedial course for students unable to write coherent sentences. These numbers seem high given the quality of the student body. The majority come from prosperous suburban high schools. The campus is ranked as "competitive" by *Barrons College Guide* (the fourth of six categories). Thus, of students admitted to this "competitive university," a quarter are unable to compose coherent paragraphs; over 3 percent are unable to compose coherent sentences. In contrast to this situation, the academic standards adopted so widely adopted by our states for K–12 curricula show that the ability to write a coherent paragraph is universally viewed as a reasonable and even modest goal to set for all high school graduates.

Philosophical Digression

In my opinion, the neglect of grammar has had other, obviously adverse effects, starting in academia but extending beyond its borders. To explain these other effects, I must first establish a point about language that will probably seem obvious to readers who are not professional academics. The point is that intelligible statements have definite literal meanings. These are fixed by the rules of language described in dictionaries and grammars. If you ask me for the literal meaning of a sentence in classical Greek, for example, you are seeking not a personal opinion but an objective truth. This is really a matter of common sense. If statements did not have definite, literal meanings, such things as those simultaneous translations at the United Nations and captions on foreign films would be impossible, as would all kinds of verbal communications requiring exact understandings—e.g., between pilots and air-traffic controllers. Nevertheless, the whole concept of literal meaning has fallen into disfavor in academia.

Doubts about literal meanings arise from a kind of confusion that characterizes much current thought in academia. Every discussion of every subject relies on concepts that draw lines between the things that they include and the things they do not. Viewed closely enough, however, few of these lines are ever perfectly clear or unambiguous. For example, our use of the cliché "different as night and day" implies that it is easy to tell night and day apart, and yet we would be hard pressed to explain exactly when night ends and day begins. Similarly, it is very difficult to say where childhood ends and adulthood begins, but I have no difficulty classifying myself, at 59, as an adult. I could not give an exact description of the northern border of Mexico or the southern border of Canada, but sitting here in Milwaukee, Wisconsin, I am sure that I am in the United States. That it is daytime as I write and that I am an adult, not a child, living in the United States, not Mexico or Canada—these are not just my personal opinions. I know that they are true as certainly as any human being can know anything.[31]

To say that intelligible statements have definite, literal meanings is like saying that countries have borders. Even though the borders may be disputed and hard, or even impossible, to ascertain with exactness, it is still possible to say with certainty of many people, buildings, and landmarks that they are or are not located in a given country at a given time. So, too, with intelligible statements. Of all the literal meanings that could be imputed to any given statement, via paraphrase, logical inference, or translation into another language, some are objectively correct, obviously inside the borders; others, obviously outside. "My dog has fleas" means that a canine creature, owned by the speaker, is infested by tiny insects. This is not my subjective interpretation of the statement. It is a correct paraphrase of the statement's literal meaning.[32]

Language has many different uses. Statements are often made for reasons other than affirming the truth of their literal meanings. My mother used to sing "My dog has fleas" when she was tuning her ukelele. She didn't even have a dog. But the use to which statements are put does not alter their literal meanings.[33]

Trying to figure out why a person says something provides an essentially different kind of mental challenge than does comprehending the literal meaning of the thing said. Put simply, there is no set procedure for discovering motives behind a statement, but procedures do exist for ascertaining literal meanings. This is a critical distinction in sorting our mental activities, one that was first made, as far as I can tell, by Immanuel Kant, in his last great essay, *Critique of Judgment* (Introduction, Part 4). Kant uses the term *judgment* to denote all of our appraisals of the external world, from adding a column of numbers to admiring a sunset. He says that there are two basic kinds of judgment. He calls them "determinate" and "reflective," respectively. We make a determinate judgment when we apply a set of rules or definitions that have been given ahead of time to particular phenomena. Clear examples of determinate judgments are those made by referees, umpires, and judges at sporting events. Reflective judgments occur when we field questions that cannot be settled by consulting rule books. At sporting events, "color commentators" specialize in reflective judgments. To answer the question of why a person made a particular remark involves reflective judgment; summarizing its literal meaning involves determinate judgment.

This distinction between determinate and reflective judgments illuminates an ambiguity in the way that we speak about the "meanings" of words and statements. Words bring many thoughts to mind in addition to those that are dictated by their literal meanings. When I hear "My dog has fleas," I always think about my mother and her ukelele, but David Mulroy's mother and ukeleles are not part of the statement's literal meaning. Such additional thoughts might be called "free associations." Of free associations, some are entirely personal and others may be very common. Maybe millions of people tune ukeleles by singing "My dog has fleas," and they think of the instrument when they hear the words. Yet, whether limited to one person or shared by millions, they are "free" associations in the sense that they are not dictated by the rules of language. Free associations are the meanings that we attach to words by use of reflective judgment in contrast to the literal meanings that are discovered through determinate judgment by applying the rules of lexicography and grammar.

Throughout the centuries, literary artists have exploited the free associations of words as well as their literal meanings. Before the twentieth century, however, literal meaning remained the chief focus of literary artists and critics. In antiquity and the middle ages, paraphrasing the literal meanings of poems was a common educational exercise. It was simply taken for granted that any poem worth reading had a literal meaning that could be paraphrased in plain prose by a competent reader and that doing so was a reasonable first step toward the complete comprehension of the poem. The practice goes back at least to the Roman teacher Quintilian. He and his successors had students express the poet's or the orator's thoughts in plain, unambiguous language. "Four score and seven years ago, our fathers brought forth upon this continent a new nation" might have become "Eighty-seven years ago, our ancestors founded a new state here in North America." Paraphrases eliminate the special aesthetic qualities of poetic and rhetorical speech. Neither Quintilian nor anyone else ever argued that paraphrases were equivalent in all respects or as good as the artistic originals. The purpose of the paraphrase is to capture and clarify determinate, literal meanings.

In modern times, a number of artists passed into a new realm. Literary works were produced that seemed to lack definite literal meanings—e.g., Joyce's *Finnegan's Wake*. There is no reason that authors should not seek aesthetic effects primarily through free associations, even at the expense of any coherent literal meaning. A problem has arisen in connection with this approach to literary art; however, it has been incorrectly used as a comprehensive model for *all* interpretation. Even works with determinate literal meanings are now commonly interpreted through free association, and the attempt to paraphrase literal meanings has been labeled a fallacy.[34]

Tonight's Seminar Topic: Why Did We Revert to Tribalism?

The tendency of modern teachers to disparage the importance of literal meanings reinforces and is reinforced by the low status of grammar, since the rules of grammar play an indispensable role in establishing the literal meanings of statements. Grammar and literal meanings have both become pariahs, and this fact lies at the root of several troubling tendencies.

To a teacher in the humanities, the most obvious of these tendencies pertains to reading comprehension. We increasingly encounter students who can speculate about the "hidden meanings" of literary texts but miss their literal sense. To gauge the extent of this problem, I recently asked members of one of my large mythology classes to produce brief paraphrases of the first sentence of the Declaration of Independence:

> When in the course of human events, it becomes necessary for one people to dissolve the political bands which have connected them with another, and to assume among the powers of the earth, the separate and equal station to which the Laws of Nature and Nature's God entitle them, a decent respect to the opinions of mankind requires that they should declare the causes which impel them to the separation.

I was looking for a restatement of the proposition expressed in the main clause, that respect for public opinion makes it necessary for parties who are abandoning an established union to explain why they are doing so. It was disconcerting that of sixty-one students who tried to paraphrase the sentence, none seemed to recognize its source. Some thought that it had to do with ending a romance. I estimated that twenty-five comprehended the gist of the sentence. In making this assessment, I tried to be fair, taking into account the fact that the students were writing extemporaneously. I counted as correct any paper that seemed to get the essential idea even when it was expressed somewhat incoherently. For example:

> When people decide to fight/separate among countries, cities, themselves, they should say why they are fighting.

> In life, people dissolve political bands that connect them with another, in order to join earth and its powers, by following Nature's and God's path, should declare why they separate.

Yet, even without nitpicking, a majority of students seemed to miss the idea altogether. For example:

> In people's lives, things may happen that would cause them to no longer want to be part of a certain government of which they are part. These things would give them reason enough to become their own ruling body.

Most disturbing, however, were a large number of students who responded to the assignment with misguided enthusiasm. It should be noticed that in many cases the students' difficulty in comprehension evidently does not arise from a deficient vocabulary.

> When dealing with events in life, one should drop preconceived knowings and assume that everything that happens, happens for a reason, and basically life goes on.

> I believe it is saying that as a group of people everyone is equal, but when it comes to laws of nature, only the strong will survive.

> Cut your earthly bonds and wear the mantle of Nature and God. Wield the power and declare justly your ascension from man's law. Then all shall bow before your might.

> Every human encounter is special and is an important piece of an intertwined quilt. Every man and god's creatures should have the respect and dignity they deserve.

> I think it means that people should look at their own morals. They should follow the laws of Nature and Nature's God, but also in their own way follow their own morals.

> As life proceeds, down to the very moment through which we perceive our existence as, indeed, separate entities of perception, transformation is key to our understanding of the necessity of change, and its living role, within all of us, in relation to time.

> People must have true facts to back up their thoughts on a god if they are different from the thoughts of the majority.

> It doesn't matter where you came from. In the end we are all human beings. Humans are at the top of the food chain, but it doesn't mean we shouldn't respect nature. Because we have one earth, learn to preserve it.

And, finally:

> I can't paraphrase this sentence because I'm not sure what point is being prevailed. Politics? Nature?[35]

I was taken aback by how poorly the students had done on this test and repeated it twice with essentially the same results. Most recently, in November 2002, I offered the paraphrase exercise as an opportunity for "extra credit" on a mythology test. Sixty-four students of 118 attempted it. Thirty-three seemed to have grasped the essential thought. Among the others were some more vivid examples of interpretation by free association. For example:

> Mankind is in a state of separation. There will come a time when all will be forgotten, and man will be one with mother earth.

> When man loses all political structure and is reverted back to tribal and instinctive nature, man should figure out what happened, so it won't happen again.

These responses seem to me to exemplify a kind of higher illiteracy. The students who suffer from this are proficient in spoken English and can express their own thoughts in writing adequately. They lack the tools, however, for the precise interpretation of the meaning of complex statements. This kind of illiteracy boils down to an ignorance of grammar. If a student interprets the first sentence of the Declaration of Independence as an exhortation to "preserve the earth," then how can you demonstrate the error? There is no way to do so that does not involve grammatical analysis: the subject of the main clause is *respect to the opinions of mankind*, the main verb is *requires*, and so forth.

America's Special Intellectual Life

> I know of no country in which, speaking generally, there is less independence of mind and true freedom of discussion than in America.
> —(Alexis de Tocqueville, *Democracy in America*)

In society at large, the same kind of a-grammatical interpretation by free association has adversely affected the quality of debate on issues of national importance and is one of the factors behind our obsession with "sensitive" language. We cannot get by in life without euphemisms. In serious matters, however, a person's words should be judged by their literal meanings, since that is the only aspect that can be determined with precision and judged to be true or false. In our times, however, so much attention is paid to the associations of individual words that our freedom of speech has been subjected to even more narrow restraints than those remarked upon by de Tocqueville. Many innocuous terms have become taboo because they are said to have painful associations for some people. Euphemistic replacements have become mandatory. The list started with genuinely hateful epithets but now includes words and expressions that future generations will never believe to have been thought objectionable. In a section on "Avoiding Insensitive and Offensive Language, the *Random House Webster's College Dictionary* (2000) proscribes the terms Oriental, Asiatic, Eskimo, and native (used as a noun). It says that people should not be referred to as "elderly, aged, or old" but as "senior citizens." The phrase "AIDS sufferer" should be replaced by "person living with AIDS." "Crazy, demented, and insane" should only be used "facetiously." And, of course, most compounds containing the suffix *-man* but denoting both men and women—e.g., "chairman"—should be avoided, although the word *woman* itself is still acceptable.

The authors note that the euphemisms *challenged, differently abled,* and *special* are "often ridiculed and best avoided." Such, of course, is the likely fate of all mandatory euphemisms. Among my students, "gay," previously an upbeat synonym for homosexual, has become an all-purpose pejorative.[36] One of them reported seeing a T-shirt with the motto "Homophobia is gay."

When we were first married, my wife and I were amused by an account that we read of life in a mental hospital. During the holidays, the staff wanted to have the patients sing Christmas carols. At first, every carol they tried touched off a violent reaction in at least one of the patients because of some word association. Finally, the staff made up a song that did not offend anybody. It went, "Christmas tree, oh Christmas tree, Christmas tree, oh Christmas tree, . . ." For years, my wife and I would sing this song when either one of us thought that the other one was looking irritable. In recent decades, American society has come to resemble that mental hospital. In fact, it is worse. Even "Christmas tree, oh Christmas tree" is out—not because of its literal meaning but because of the religious intolerance that could quite possibly motivate the singing of it.

Our fixation with the associations of our words rather than the literal meanings of statements also results in exaggerated concern with the labeling of political positions. We are all painfully aware that representatives of either side of the abortion controversy attach great importance to being called "pro-life" and "pro-choice," as though an opinion's name matters more than its substance. In a more intelligent culture, they would use neutral, mutually acceptable terms for their respective beliefs and debate their logical underpinnings. Again, the disputed election of 2000 raised some interesting and complicated issues. Rather than airing them in a civil way, candidate Gore repeated that he just wanted the votes to be "counted," while candidate Bush shot back that the votes had already been "counted" repeatedly. What lay behind the exchange, of course, was a not particularly elusive ambiguity in the word "count." Ideally, our two aspiring leaders would have been able to define their real differences in mutually acceptable terms and air them civilly and articulately. Instead, each tried to cloak himself in the favorable associations of the words *count* and *vote* used in rapid succession.

By far the worst effect of interpretation by free association, however, is the legitimation of *ad hominem* arguments. Of all the associations that are attached to statements by reflective judgments, those having to do with the speaker's or the author's motives are the most common. In a culture in which interpretation is typically based on free association, people have inevitably lost sight of the fact that speculation about motives is an invalid method of argumentation, a well-known logical fallacy. I distinctly remember my first encounter with this principle when I began debating in high school. Our coach explained that a debate concerned the merits of a proposition—e.g., "Should the village replace its bridge?" The question was whether the benefits of replacing the bridge would exceed the costs. In arguing the case, the character of one's opponent made no difference. The affirmative side might be represented by a neo-Nazi, Satanist pedophile who owned a bridge-building company. It just did not matter. As *Robert's Rules of Order* puts it, debate concerns the measure, not the man. Either the village needs a new bridge, or it does not. The merits of the proposition do not depend on the motives or character of its advocates or its opponents. This made perfectly good sense to me as a high school freshman, and it still does. Nevertheless, this simple, obvious, elementary principle has ceased to be common wisdom. In every heated public debate, aspersions are routinely cast on the motives of advocates on either side. Both critics and defenders of "affirmative action" are called "racists" by their opponents. People on either side of the controversies over tax rates, abortion, and capital punishment are accused of harboring deplorable attitudes. Most discouraging, however, is the fact that new state academic standards in the language arts actually encourage students to engage in *ad hominem* arguments. In Wisconsin, for example, a standard for grade 12 under the heading of

"Effective Participation in Discussion" reads: "Detect and evaluate a speaker's bias." And later: "Appraise the purpose of discussion by examining their context and the motivation of participants." California's Listening and Speaking Standards for grade 8 include this: "Evaluate the credibility of a speaker (e.g., hidden agendas, slanted or biased material)." In Kansas, fifth-graders are supposed to perceive an author's "purpose"; eighth-graders, his "point of view"; eleventh-graders, his "point of view or bias."

This is not the way to train students to participate in serious discussions. Charges of hidden agendas or biases and raising the question of motives are sure ways to turn conversations into shouting matches. Students should be exhorted, when engaged in serious discussion, to analyze the meaning of statements according to the rules of lexicography and grammar and then to test their truthfulness according to the rules of logic and evidence, while disregarding extraneous associations. One arrives at truth and maintains civility by obeying well-grounded rules, not through exhortations to be sensitive and certainly not by trying to psychoanalyze one's opponent. We cannot have good conversations in our society unless we attend to the literal meanings of what we say to one another, and we cannot do that without greater emphasis on understanding grammar.

Or so it seems to me. The gist of my argument so far has been that America's academic and intellectual life has been adversely affected by our educational establishment's policy of opposition to formal instruction in grammar. Conversely, I hold that education would be improved if students in the early grades—fourth through sixth, say—learned the parts of speech, how to conjugate verbs, and other basic grammatical concepts thoroughly and carefully. Doing so would take energy away from other activities. The net educational gain would not necessarily be visible immediately. In my opinion, it would show up eventually, in high school and college. Trying to establish this hypothesis scientifically, however, would involve a long-term experiment with large, matched sets of students. This is not something that a humble Classics professor has the resources or expertise to arrange. In fact, the best hope for massive empirical evidence in favor of teaching grammar in the early grades lies in England's current reform. Yet, even such a large-scale experiment will not necessarily produce decisive results. Unlike medical experiments, educational ones are almost inevitably skewed by the attitudes of researchers and subjects. The British experiment could be undermined by resistance from teachers, who are being subjected to mandatory retraining, or made to succeed by the ephemeral zeal of its champions. Then, too, the evaluation of educational experiments is often clouded by disagreements over what exactly constitutes an educational gain.

Empirical research has an important role to play in educational debates, but its difficulties and ambiguities mean that there is also need for supplementary kinds of evidence and argumentation. Specifically, I think that it is imperative at this juncture that language arts educators pause to consider the story of grammar in education, in order to put their current policy of neglect into a historical perspective. In my opinion, doing so will make it clear that formal instruction in grammar deserves a careful second look. As an academic practice, the teaching of grammar has a long and honorable history; the arguments used to justify its abandonment do not withstand much scrutiny.

Notes

1. Wallace, 41, footnote 4.

2. Herbert Stahlke, *Re: subordinate clauses as mains clauses*, [*ATEG@LISTSERV. MUOHIO.EDU.*] Dec. 4, 2000. The passive voice in English is formed with the appropriate tense of the verb *be* and the past participle of a transitive verb—e.g., "(Mistakes) were made." Students who lack systematic knowledge of the forms of *be*—as most do—and do not know what a past participle is are naturally mystified by the term and conclude that the term *passive* is used of sentences in which the subjects do not exert themselves. Hence, as Professor Stahlke observed, they (and some of their teachers) end up classifying sentences that speak of experiences—e.g., "I feel your pain"—as passive.

3. In Part I of the test, the sixteen students were ask to choose the part of speech (noun, pronoun, adjective, verb, adverb, conjunction, preposition, interjection) of the word printed in bold type. The number in parentheses represents correct answers out of sixteen. 1. The fans were all clapping **enthusiastically.** (9, adverb) 2. I'd like a **juicy** steak. (11, adjective) 3. The dog ran across the **street.** (13, noun) 4. I was stranded in Copenhagen **without** a cent. (5, preposition) 5. He **organizes** laundry workers. (11, verb) 6. **Yikes!** My foot is on fire. (9, interjection) 7. I have decided to volunteer **because** I love my country. (7, conjunction) 8. Jack grabbed the ball and threw **it** into the river. (8, pronoun) 9. He is **rather** charming, isn't he? (4, adverb) 10. **Am** I really your son? (3, verb)? 11. This is a case of **murder.** (7, noun) 12. Your breath smells **awful.** (9, adjective)

   In Part II, students were asked to exemplify various grammatical phenomena from the following sentences: 1. Black Widows are feared by everyone. 2. Cholera kills many people in the third world every year. 3. Expatriates are often too bitter to return home. 4. Hand Henry the Hollandaise sauce. 5. Fortunately, the king has rescinded the order. The examples sought and the number of correct answers were as follows: a noun used as a direct object of a verb, 3; a noun used as the subject of a sentence, 10; a noun used as the object of a preposition, 1; a verb in the passive voice, 3; a verb in the imperative mood, 4; a prepositional phrase, 4; a verb in a perfect tense, 1; a noun used as an indirect object, 2; an infinitive, 1.

4. Pinker, 290–93.

5. Published in *Proceedings of the Modern Language Association* XL (1925): 963–1024.

6. Hillocks and Smith, 592.

7. Fries, 1–2.

8. See note 1 in Preface, xiii.

9. Braddock (1963) 37–38.

10. Kolln 2001, 5–6.

11. Hillocks and Smith, 596.

12. Elbow, 169.

13. Weaver, 144–45.

14. E.g., [*lists.asu.edu/cgi-bin/wa?A2=ind0206&L=wpa-l&P=R28625.*] Jan. 19, 2003.

15. Martha Kolln, *Understanding English Grammar.* Six editions have now been published. The first four—1982, 1986, 1990, and 1994—published by Macmillan, a 1998 edition from Allyn and Bacon, and a 2002 edition by Longman. The two most recent editions include the work of a co-author, Robert Funk. Kolln is also the author of *Rhetorical Grammar: Grammatical Choices, Rhetorical Effects.*

16. The printed version is cited above (note 9). I have drawn on this speech heavily in composing this chapter.

17. Sum et al., 30.

18. Ravitch, 517, footnote 6.

19. Murray and Herrnstein, 44–46.

20. Ravitch, 517, footnote 6.

21. Omar Johnstone, "Is direct grammar instruction needed in grade school?" a posting on the ATEG List, [*ATEG@LISTSERV.MUOHIO.EDU.*] Sept. 17, 2001.

22. Brod and Welles, 25.

23. Statistics cited in this paragraph are taken from Brod and Welles (1998) supplemented by LaFleur (1992), Brod (1975), and the Digest of Education Statistics published by the U.S. Department of Health Education and Welfare (1965, 1969). As gleaned from these sources, total enrollments in U.S. institutions of higher education have grown as follows: 3,789,000 (1960); 5,920,864 (1965); 7,513,0901 (1968); 8,580,887 (1970); 12,096,895 (1980); 13,818,637 (1990); 14,261,781 (1995); and 14,590,000 (1998). Enrollments in various foreign languages in absolute numbers and as a percentage of total enrollments are as follow: Classical Greek, 1960: 12,700 (.3%); 1965: 19,500 (.3%); 1970: 16,697 (.2%); 1980: 22,111 (.2%); 1990: 16,401 (.1%); 1995: 16,272 (.1%); 1998: 16,402 (.1%). French, 1960: 228,813 (6%); 1968: 388,096 (5%); 1970: 359,313 (4%); 1980: 248,361 (2%); 1995: 205,351 (1%); 1998: 199,064 (1%). German,

1960: 146,116 (4%); 1968: 216,263 (2%); 1970: 202,569 (2%); 1980: 126,910 (1%); 1990: 133,348 (.9%); 1995: 96,263 (.6%); 1998: 89,020 (.6%). Latin, 1960: 25,700 (.7%); 1965: 39,600 (.7%); 1970: 27,591 (.3%); 1980: 25,035 (.2%); 1990: 28,178 (.2%); 1995: 25,897 (.2%); 1998: 26,145 (.2%). Russian, 1960: 30,570 (.8%); 1968: 40,696 (.5%); 1970: 36,189 (.4%); 1980: 23,987 (.2%); 1990: 44,626 (.3%); 1995: 24,729 (.2%); 1998: 23,791 (.2%). Spanish, 1960: 178,689 (5%); 1968: 364,870 (5%); 1970: 389,150 (4.5%); 1980: 379,379 (3%); 1990: 533,944 (4%); 1995: 606,286 (4%); 656,590 (4.5%); 1998.

24. Schulz, 285.

25. Cp. Tucker, 53: "Since the early 1980's, research in foreign language acquisition and pedagogy has stressed the importance of a student-centered, communicative classroom environment in which the learner is encouraged to explore in a meaningful way the target language and various cultural phenomena that are associated with it."

26. Schneider and Von der Emde, 18.

27. The study of grammar has also been discouraged by educational experts in England in recent decades. The results are reported by Melanie Phillips, *All Must Have Prizes* (Little, Brown, 1996). She quotes (7–8) an article by John Gordon, a tutor of foreign languages at East Anglia University. He reports on a test given to first-year students who had excellent or above-average grades in German in high school. Few could translate simple English sentences into German. For example, only eight of forty-three answered "The teacher gave the pupil the book" correctly. Gordon commented, "This sentence was once widely used to introduce learners to the use of the indirect object. Until recently the use of this sentence in a test after the first year or so of German would have been regarded as some kind of jest; and its inclusion in any sort of post A-level test at university or anywhere else would have been quite unthinkable; it would have been regarded as an insult to the students."

28. Karen Heise, "Freshman (De)Composition: The Results of Grammar's Slow Death in the College Classroom," *Academic Exchange (An Online Forum for Educators and Students)*, Sept. 7, 2001. [*asccsa.unco.edu/students/AE-Extra/2001/8/index.html*.] Dec. 30, 2002.

29. "College Remediation: What It Is, What It Costs, What's at Stake," Institute for Higher Education Policy, December 1998, p. vii.

30. These statistics were provided by Erl Olfe, assistant dean, College of Letters and Science, University of Wisconsin-Milwaukee.

31. Cp. Searle, 102: "It is not necessarily an objection to a conceptual analysis, or to a distinction, that there are no rigorous or precise boundaries to the concept analyzed or the distinction being drawn. . . . This is something of a cliché in analytic philosophy: most concepts and distinctions are rough at the edges and do not have sharp boundaries. The distinctions between fat and thin, rich and poor, democracy and authoritarianism, for example, do not have sharp boundaries."

32. Cp. Searle, 126: "When I complain about the heat or order a hamburger, I am, in general, able to do so without ambiguity or vagueness, much less indeterminacy. Within the constraints set by the condition of the possibility on the speech act, I can say what I want to say and mean what I want to mean."

33. Searle, 110, uses the terms "sentence meaning" and "speaker meaning" to make the same distinction. His example is "The window is open." This sentence has one obvious literal, or sentence, meaning; but it could be used with any number of different speaker's meanings—e.g., as a polite request to close the window or metaphorically of the presence of some opportunity. Searle also believes that the failure to make this distinction has caused considerable confusion in literary studies.

34. The locus classicus is the final chapter of Cleanth Brooks's *The Well-Wrought Urn*, "The Heresy of the Paraphrase." Brooks's presentation is fundamentally confused. It must be remembered that the paraphrase in the traditional sense of the term, as used by Quintilian, for example, referred to a word-by-word translation of poetry or oratory into normal language. "Four score and seven" becomes "eighty-seven," for example. The traditional paraphrase has roughly the same number of words as the original text, sometimes many more. In disparaging the practice of "paraphrase," Brooks disregards this traditional meaning of the term. He uses it instead to denote a summary statement of the supposed, logical implications of a poem, like an abstract of a research paper. For example, he offers as a "paraphrase" of Wordsworth's *Intimations Ode* the statement that it "celebrates the spontaneous 'naturalness' of the child" and points out that this does not do justice to the complexity of the poem. He thus reduces the "literal meaning" of a work to a motto that could be distilled from it—on this view, the "literal" meaning of the *Iliad* might be that war is bad—and argues that the broad, connotative meeting is more important than such literal meanings. In all of this, a crucial distinction was lost. The *literal* meaning of a text in the traditional sense of the word would be an exhaustive compilation of the logical meanings of each of its sentences as objectively determined by the lexicon and grammar of the language involved. .

    Literal meanings should be of special concern to literary scholars, since only texts have literal meanings and since ascertaining them involves the making of determinate judgments for which special training is sometimes required. Like all entities, texts can also function as the occasions for reflection. In creating the aesthetic effects for which they are valued, the literal meanings and broader meanings of a literary text are inextricably intertwined—i.e, the text with its literal meaning properly understood becomes an occasion for reflection. If we do not understand the literal meaning of a literary text, then we cannot really claim to be responding to it *as literature* when we reflect upon it, because literal meaning is the distinctive characteristic of literature in the realm of art.

    Despite the superficiality of its treatment of the venerable practice of paraphrase, Brooks's essay has been immensely influential. As far as I can ascertain, no major critic since the era of The New Criticism has discussed literal meaning, except to derogate its importance.

35. Ken Weinig, the headmaster of the Independence School in Newark, Delaware, suggested the use of this sentence as a litmus test of grammatical competence. The class involved was an introduction to classical mythology, taught at the University of Wisconsin-Milwaukee in the fall of 2000. The class is a popular means for students to fulfill humanities requirements and is taken by a cross-section of undergraduates. The papers on which I collected these responses contained a line for the student's name, the heading "Special Research Exercise," and the following instructions: "Please write out a brief summary or paraphrase of the statement below. Try to express essentially the same thought more concisely. Limit your paraphrase to thirty-five words. I am giving you this exercise in connection with some of my own research. I will explain its purpose in a later class. All students who turn in a paper containing a good-faith effort to follow directions will be given two extra credit points on their first test. Authors of what I classify as excellent paraphrases will be given five points."

36. *The Weekly Standard*, Aug. 13, 2001, p. 2, reported that the media director of the Gay and Lesbian Alliance Against Defamation had condemned the movie *Jay and Silent Bob Strike Back* because its protagonists "substitute the word 'gay' for something that is wrong or stupid."

Chapter Two

The First Liberal Art

Why Do We Always Start with the Greeks?

Grammar entered education in the West as the first and most important of the seven liberal arts. These in turn represented a distillation of the great gains achieved through alphabetic literacy.

When I was a student, the fundamental importance of the ancient Greeks and Romans in many fields was taken for granted. Soon after I started teaching, however, the question of why they were given so much attention began to arise with increasing urgency, and I felt impelled to seek an answer. The answer I found was one of stark simplicity. It is that the Greeks invented the alphabet—and the Romans were among the first to borrow it.

The importance of the alphabet is not fully appreciated even in academia. People often misinterpret what I have to say on this point. Lest there be any confusion, I am not saying that the Greeks invented writing. Many peoples knew how to write before the Greeks. The Greek alphabet, however, is a system of writing of revolutionary accuracy and simplicity. Our alphabet is the same as the Greeks' with minor modifications. As I compose this essay on a computer, I am using an invention of the twentieth century A.D. together with one of the eighth century B.C.

Writing systems that preceded the alphabet were more complicated and used only by professional scribes. Cuneiform writing employs three to four hundred signs; Egyptian hieroglyphics, over six hundred. Before the invention of the alphabet and an intervening dark age, the Greeks themselves used a syllabic system of writing called Linear B with approximately ninety signs.

Just before the invention of the Greek alphabet, Semitic tribes, the ancestors of the Arabs and Jews, were the leaders in literacy in the

28

Mediterranean world. They had a simple prototypical alphabet with slightly more than twenty acrophontic signs—i.e., ones that stood for the sounds with which syllables began, consonants in our terms. The rest, the vowel sounds, had to be inferred from context. This was enough for writing traditional songs, when it was only necessary to jog a reader's memory. It was also adequate in contexts requiring simple ideas—e.g., lists of merchandise. It was not, however, ideal for recording complicated, original ideas.[1]

The Greeks got the idea of the alphabet from the Phoenicians, Semites who were the leaders in navigation and international trade during the dark age, the inhabitants of modern Lebanon. The Greeks borrowed Phoenician signs to represent their own consonants. They also used several, which were not needed for Greek consonants, to symbolize pure Greek vowel sounds. In this way, consonant signs ceased being abbreviations for various syllables. They became abstractions standing for configurations of lip and tongue and methods of vocalization used to modify vowel sounds. This is the ingenious innovation that underlies the alphabet. It led to a system of twenty-four signs that accurately represented human speech, a system so simple that children could and did master it easily, by learning what is now called *phonics*. Another Wisconsin classicist, Barry B. Powell, has done extensive research on the invention of the alphabet. He dates it to 800 B.C. and attributes it to a Greek from Euboea, an area of Greece that was in contact with Phoenician traders during that period.[2]

To understand the impact of the alphabet, one needs to know a little about Greek civilization before its appearance. A few centuries earlier, about 1200 B.C., the Greeks had reached a cultural peak. Their kings lived in citadels with monumental walls. Golden crowns and funeral masks and daggers with inlaid gold and silver have been retrieved from their royal tombs. The archeological record suggests that their armies were powerful enough to conquer the island of Crete. Within a hundred years, however, for reasons unknown, this civilization collapsed, and Greece experienced a dark age. There is no evidence of monumental architecture or of art worthy of the name in the centuries following the collapse. No form of writing survives. There is no evidence of large or prosperous cities. Incredibly, the entire population of one of the principal dark-age settlements excavated by archeologists, that at Lefkandi on the island of Euboea, is estimated at twenty-five at its height in the ninth century. Greek civilization was dying. Its trajectory was parallel with that of the Hittites, another Indo-European people who had a flourishing bronze-age civilization that also collapsed around 1100 B.C.

Hittite civilization did die, but in the wake of the invention of the alphabet, Greek civilization made an amazing comeback. It does not seem to me that this is surprising. We take alphabetic literacy for granted, but think what an invention it was. People in general thereby gained the ability to step outside of their streams of consciousness, freeze them, examine them, edit them, and make generalized observations about their content. The thoughts of others could now be examined in the same way, as could all the stories, songs, and proverbs that had hitherto been experienced only via nonstop oral transmission. In short, the Greek invention of the alphabet made the static representation of thought widely accessible. Merely by considering its nature, one would expect that alphabetic literacy would occasion a quantum leap in intellectual analysis and communication. The empirical evidence is fully consistent with this conjecture.

The most familiar evidence of the benefits of alphabetic literacy consists of the series of innovative literary masterpieces that materialized in its wake.[3] The series begins with Homer's epic poems. They show unmistakable signs of originating in an oral tradition but are far superior in literary quality to any known examples of purely oral poetry. This means that Homer was an oral poet, but an oral poet with an edge, with some distinctive advantage over other oral poets. Although expert opinion on the role of the alphabet in the creation of his poems remains divided, the inference seems unavoidable that he profited from its invention in one way or another. If he himself did not learn how to use it, he may have taken advantage of the service of a scribe in the process of revising and organizing his monumental works.[4]

The most remarkable thing about Greek literature in Homer's wake is its rapid evolution. Each successive generation mastered new genres. First came personal lyric poems by Sappho and others and choral songs best represented by Pindar. In less than a century, the choral songs evolved into Greek tragedy and comedy. Prose literature emerged in the histories of Herodotus and Thucydides and the philosophical works of Plato and Aristotle. Even if alphabetic literacy were somehow not the cause of the proliferation and high quality of the poetic genres, there could be no doubt that Greek history and philosophy owed their existence to it. Oral cultures preserve "texts" by casting them into poetic form, whose rhythms facilitate memorization. Hence, a paradoxical fact: poetry precedes prose in the evolution of literature, even though the latter is easier to write. Poetic texts like Homer's are the remnants of an oral culture. Prose works like Herodotus' history, and Plato's dialogues presuppose literacy.

After the invention of the alphabet, the Greeks made comparable advances in other fields. By 600 B.C., the Mediterranean world was dotted with prosperous Greek city-states that dominated the areas in which they were located. They were found on the coast of modern Turkey, the shore of the Black Sea, the islands of the Aegean, Sicily, southern France, southern

Italy, and northern Africa. Athenian democracy evolved from experimentation with the governance of city-states, in which written laws and constitutions played a role. A people whose arts and architecture were unremarkable in 900 B.C., the Greeks produced the Parthenon and classical sculpture in the fifth century. Military nonentities in 900, they repelled an invasion by the Persian Empire at the beginning of the fifth century and then in the fourth invaded and conquered that empire under the leadership of Alexander the Great. Greek military dominance rested on an intellectual and technological foundation. On land, the Greeks had hoplites, infantry soldiers wearing bronze armor who were carefully trained to fight in formation. On sea, the fast, maneuverable Greek triremes powered by three banks of expert oarsmen made other battleships obsolete.

At present, Classical scholars are apt to emphasize the limits of early Greek literacy and the ways in which it differed from its modern counterpart. As far we can tell, the Greeks did not have easy access to writing materials. Communication must have remained primarily oral; the majority of the population, illiterate. Written works were written in order to be read aloud. Nevertheless, the evidence suggests that enough Greeks took advantage of alphabetic literacy to achieve what has been called a "tipping point" in other contexts. The record is unambiguous: Greek culture was suddenly transformed by a remarkable series of advances in numerous fields shortly after the alphabet appeared; advances in literature led the way. Surely, the alphabet played a critical role.[5]

During Alexander's life, the Romans had just begun to make their presence felt in the western Mediterranean. It is hardly a coincidence that these people who would supplant the Greeks as the dominant power in the Mediterranean were also among the first to adapt the Greek alphabet to their own language. In fact, the eagerness with which the Romans emulated the Greeks' literary accomplishments is one of the most remarkable facts of ancient history. Rome gained political dominance in the western Mediterranean by its hard-fought victory over Carthage in the Second Punic War (218–201 B.C.). At that time, the effort to assimilate Greek literary culture was well underway. Rome's first known author, a Greek slave named Livius Andronicus, had translated the *Odyssey* and a selection of Greek tragedies into Latin several decades before the war began. The first Roman to gain lasting literary fame, Plautus, flourished during it, producing comedies loosely adapted from Greek models but unmistakably Roman in their underlying spirit. He was roughly contemporary with Ennius, a prolific Italian author, who produced an epic poem on Rome's history and many other works, and with the famous Roman statesman, Cato the Elder, who left 150 orations, a history of Rome, and numerous essays on special topics. We assume that conquerors will impose their cultures on the vanquished. It is a tribute to the uncanny practicality of the Romans that they did exactly the opposite, conquering Greece and Hellenizing themselves with equal zeal. And the Romans were aware of the irony. Horace, in *Epistles* (2.1.156), writes: *Graecia capta ferum victorem cepit* ("In captivity, Greece captivated her fierce victor").

Rome's ability to appreciate and absorb Greek culture was evidently one of the keys to its dynamism. It was not shared by Rome's rivals, the Etruscans or Carthaginians, neither of whom produced the equivalent of a Plautus. The Carthaginians retained a Phoenician script. The Second Punic War was a close contest. The fact that Roman dispatches had vowels may have had an effect on the outcome.

Seven Divine Bridesmaids

The last stage of ancient Greek history is known as the Hellenistic period, when the conquests of Alexander the Great had spread Greek culture over all of the Near East. The Greeks of the Hellenistic period and the Romans who rose to political dominance during this time had the highest possible regard for the intellectual achievements of the earlier Greeks, starting with Homer. Egypt was ruled by a Macedonian dynasty that came to power in the wake of Alexander's conquests. Its kings founded and maintained the great library at Alexandria, whose main purpose was the preservation and study of earlier Greek literature. Our texts of classical Greek literature are as good as they are because of the work of the scholars of Alexandria and others like them. Virtually all Hellenistic rulers patronized similar efforts. As far as the Romans were concerned, being educated meant studying Greek literature and philosophy. Their national epic, Virgil's *Aeneid*, is an homage to Homer.

Among the earlier Greeks, young boys were taught to read and write, but higher education lacked formality. In classical Athens, some wealthy youths paid sophists for training in speech and debate, while others achieved the same end by conversing with Socrates, but neither activity was standard behavior. As a general rule, education meant participation in the life of a city-state according to one's rank and station. Formal educational schemes evolved in the Hellenistic and Roman worlds when the appreciation of the earlier Greek achievements required more conscious effort and formal programs of study.

We do not possess continuous or comprehensive accounts of the curricula of ancient schools. Instead, scattered allusions and a few extant literary works provide snapshots of education at different periods. Several anecdotes show that it was a commonplace in the

Academy, the school established by Plato, that students could not master philosophy unless they had first completed a basic curriculum, called *enkuklios paideia* ("rounded education," whence the term "encyclopedia").[6] The subjects covered were grammar, rhetoric, logic, arithmetic, geometry, harmony, and astronomy.

The Romans imitated this curriculum, referring to the subjects studied as the *artes liberales*, "the liberal arts."[7] We know that they were studied in Republican Rome from references to a book by Marcus Terentius Varro, Rome's leading intellectual in the era of Julius Caesar. One of his many lost works was a treatise on education called *Disciplinarum Novem Libri* ("The Nine Disciplines"), which contained his reflections on the seven liberal arts plus two professional fields, medicine and architecture.

In the early fourth century A.D., Martianus Capella wrote another nine-volume work on education, *De Nuptiis Philologiae et Mercurii* ("The Marriage of Philology and Mercury"). It is an allegorical work describing the deification of Philology, who represents learning in general, and her marriage to Mercury as the personification of eloquence. The wedding is followed by the speeches of seven bridesmaids, each representing and expounding one of the seven liberal arts. The work achieved a great vogue and remained an educational classic for centuries. In keeping with its prescriptions, the standard curriculum consisted of the seven liberal arts, which were divided between the language arts of the "trivium" (grammar, logic, rhetoric) and the mathematical disciplines of the quadrivium (arithmetic, geometry, music, and astronomy). Capella lived in Roman Carthage. It is doubtful that his personal authority carried much weight. Apparently, his work achieved and retained canonical status because it embodied the conventional wisdom.

To modern eyes, Capella's work is an unreadable amalgam of mythology, Platonic allegories, and academic trivia. Yet, it endowed the liberal arts with a prestige that has lasted to the present day. Educators still pay lip service, at least, to the value of a "liberal education," but the meaning of the term has shifted in an interesting way. Focusing on the fact that the liberal arts were always distinct from narrow, pre-professional training—e.g., Varro's medicine and architecture—educators have increasingly applied the term *liberal* to all interdisciplinary courses, viz., those that are broader in scope than any of the traditional disciplines. In fact, there are now more than a hundred graduate programs in "liberal studies," whose essential component is the interdisciplinary seminar.[8] While there is nothing intrinsically wrong with, and much to be said for, interdisciplinary seminars, they have no historical claim to the use of the title "liberal arts."

What actually set the "seven liberal arts" apart in the eyes of the ancients? Why do we still instinctively value what they represent?

It must be borne in mind that the liberal arts tradition is a direct descendant of the invention of alphabetic literacy, which made static representations of thought easy to produce and maintain. By studying them, one could discover thought's basic patterns, which are what bind the seven liberal arts together. In contemporary terms, their subjects are the procedures that are hard-wired in our brains and do not differ from topic to topic. For this reason, too, the liberal arts are relatively independent of empirical observation. They can be learned largely through introspection. This fact is clearest in the cases of logic, arithmetic, and geometry. In one of his famous dialogues, "The Meno," Plato depicts Socrates leading an uneducated slave boy to the discovery of the Pythagorean theorem by asking him a series of questions. All of the doctrines of logic and mathematics could be discovered in the same way. They depend by definition on the mind's a priori knowledge.

This quality explains the special prestige enjoyed by the liberal arts. Its subjects are the rules that *seem* to be innate. Plato's Socrates maintains that such a priori truths are remembered by the soul from a glorious prenatal existence in a higher realm. It is impossible to tell how seriously Socrates or Plato took this doctrine, but it dramatizes the fact that our knowledge of what seem to be a priori truths is one of the great mysteries of the human condition. As important and honorable as the practice of medicine is, it does not share in this mystique because its basic truths cannot be discovered by introspection. Through Socratic questioning, Meno's slave boy could be led to the discovery of the Pythagorean theorem, but no amount of questioning would enable him to discover the location of the liver. For that, he would have to look. To Capella, medicine was not one of learning's divine bridesmaids because its truths relied on the observation of facts here on earth. The same was true of other respected disciplines, such as architecture and law.

All of the liberal arts lay claim to relative freedom from empirical study. As Plato makes clear in *The Republic,* he recommends the study of astronomy because it concerns universal laws governing solids in motions, not because he thinks that stars, which are just material things, are divine. By the same token, the study of harmony concerned the mathematical relationships among different tones, not familiarity with particular tunes. Harmony and astronomy were included in the curriculum as the principal subdivisions of mathematics after arithmetic and geometry. In a modern liberal arts curriculum, they would be replaced by algebra and calculus.

Rhetoric is, in one sense, the least respectable of the liberal arts. Plato argued in the *Gorgias* that it is directed at the pleasant, not necessarily the good. It is thus a knack for gratifying the appetites of others, not a true art, and stands in the relationship to the implementation of justice as cosmetics does to callisthenics or cooking does to medicine. Despite this criticism, rhetoric has always had a prominent place in the liberal arts curriculum, possibly because its utilitarian value is so obvious. Rhetoric's ancient defenders admitted that it was often misused, but they took the position intimated by Plato in the *Phaedrus* and developed by Quintilian (1 *Preface* 11–13; 2.20) that *true* rhetoric was anchored in the soul's understanding of justice and other virtues and that its seeds were planted in us by nature.

In contrast, the value of grammar was never challenged. Though our knowledge of the grammar of any given language obviously comes from experience, we acquire an intuitive understanding of our mother tongue with remarkable ease as young children. Once we become competent in a language, we can test statements about grammar by introspection rather than by empirical observation. It is as though the grammar of a particular language fleshes out abstract patterns that have the status of a priori rules in our minds. In fact, this is the position taken by Chomsky and his followers in modern linguistics. The inclusion of grammar among the liberal arts shows that even in antiquity scholars generally sensed its kinship with logic and mathematics. Its primacy among the liberal arts reflects a fact emphasized by Aristotle: truth and falsehood can be attributed only to words organized by the rules of grammar into subjects and predicates. Not even in the privacy of one's own thoughts is it possible to conceive of a truth without at least the implicit use of grammar.

In brief, the liberal arts are the disciplines whose distinctive, foundational truths are granted a priori. They seem to contradict the notion that the human intellect starts out as a *tabula rasa*. One does not have to believe in innate knowledge in order to place special value on such truths, however. Even if they are acquired entirely though nurture and experience, they deserve their special status as foundational subjects, since they are the ground rules. The entire intellectual realm is accessible to the person who has mastered grammar, logic, rhetoric (perhaps), and the principal fields of mathematics.

Though the liberal arts are thus exalted in one sense, they are humble in another sense. This point is extremely important. The liberal arts are the ground rules of thought, not its end. In Aristotelian terms, they are not speculative disciplines, aimed at learning ultimate truths, but practical ones designed to serve ulterior purposes. Their value is instrumental.

This is a point made emphatically by the fourth-century B.C. Greek orator, Isocrates. The liberal arts, he says, do not by themselves make students better speakers or counselors, just *eumathesteroi,* "better learners."[9]

Students should spend some time on them and then move along to more serious endeavors. Those who linger too long end up as mere skeletons, stranded on the subtleties of the ancient sophists. The Roman Seneca devotes a long, witty epistle (88) to the same theme[10], which he sums up in a few words. We should not be learning (*non discere debemus*) the liberal arts, he says; we should *have* learned (*didicisse*) them. The point is also implicit in Capella's allegory. The liberal arts are not learning itself, but learning's bridesmaids. These ancient warnings are prophetic. As we shall see, the elevation of one or another of the liberal arts to an end in itself is a recurring problem in education.

As a practical discipline, grammar has two, closely related goals. It preserves and perfects understanding of the great literature of the past, and it contributes to eloquent self-expression. These goals are intertwined in that an essential part of eloquence in any language is the prudent use of the models of the past. Thus, in the Greek world, grammar was originally grounded in the love of Homer and other early masterpieces, but the leading experts in preserving and interpreting their texts, men like Callimachus and Apollonius of Rhodes, were also the most renowned poets of the day.

It is not a peculiarity of the Greeks that grammar looked in this specific way both to the past, to preserve great literature, and to the future, to produce it. In India, the study of grammar was begun as a way of preserving the Vedic hymns and came to regulate the creation of classical Sanskrit poetry.[11] Similarly, the formal study of grammar was introduced into the Islamic world in the eighth century A.D. to preserve the language of the Koran and became the launching pad for the golden age of Islamic literature.[12] As we shall see, the utility of grammar in preserving the appreciation of the old classics and fostering new eloquence is also one of the great lessons of the European Renaissance. Contemporary American educators who claim to be mystified by the importance attached to grammar in some circles are overlooking quite a bit of history.

A Great Booklet

No matter how well attuned you may to the secret harmonies of nature, you will not get very far as a naturalist without knowing the difference between birds and insects. The understanding of complex phenomena begins with taxonomy. Language's basic taxonomic groups are referred to as "parts of speech."

To communicate thoughts, we must arrange words into sentences, which consist of subjects and predicates. Further distinctions may be made among the words on the basis of their specific roles in the structure of a sentence, their meanings, and the kind of changes that their forms undergo. As in any practical taxonomy, however, limits must be placed on the number of distinctions that one uses for classification. Otherwise, subdivision would continue until each word occupied its own unique category. Long experience with a number of different languages has shown that the subdivision of words into eight major groups gives people a good, practical understanding of sentence structure and "morphology," or alterations in the forms of words. This taxonomy is the nucleus of traditional grammar. A person is probably competent in the traditional grammar of a given language if he or she can identify the part of speech of each word in a normal sentence.

The limits placed on subdivision are illustrated by the use of the term *verb* in traditional grammar. A verb is the part of speech that introduces a predicate. Semantically, it is said to denote an action or a state of being, but this definition is of dubious value since nouns also denote actions and states of being. More precise is Aristotle's observation that verbs have tenses: their forms tell us whether they refer to actions or states as occurring in the present, the past, or the future. Verbs are typically also set apart by the other kinds of alterations that their forms may undergo. For example, in English, the suffix *-ing* may be added to most verbs.

Like the other parts of speech, verbs are susceptible to further subdivision. In English, the words *can, could, may, might, shall, should, will,* and *would* are traditionally grouped with verbs despite some deviant characteristics. Among these, they cannot receive the suffix *-ing*. Furthermore, they do not denote actions or states by themselves but must be followed by some other verb in its infinitive form to produce a complete predicate. Critics of traditional grammar sometimes cite facts such as these as an indication that traditional grammar is misguided, saying that these words are not verbs but "auxiliaries" and that there are, therefore, at least nine parts of speech. In fact, one could break the category of *verb* down into other subgroups—e.g., some verbs require direct objects, others do not. The point missed by such criticism is that the purpose of the taxonomy is practical guidance, not theoretical exactitude. The division of words into eight parts of speech is like the division of the world into seven continents, a matter of convention and convenience. The proof of such taxonomies' value lies in their widespread acceptance and use, and few can compete in this regard with the eight parts of speech.

The individual responsible for first dividing words into eight groups is known to posterity as Dionysius Thrax ("the Thracian"). Though Dionysius lived and worked in the Greek-speaking Hellenistic world created by the conquests of Alexander the Great, his father is said to have hailed from Thrace, the barbarian land on its northern frontier.

Little else is known about his life. He studied under Aristarchus, the head of the library of Alexandria and the greatest of literary scholars in the second century B.C. Later he taught grammar and literature on the island of Rhodes, another center of Greek intellectual life. There he did the usual thing for a professional scholar, publishing a number of treatises on language and literature. Of these, only a very brief one survives, *Techne Grammatike* ("The Grammatical Art"). Despite its brevity, it is reasonable to list Dionysius' *Techne* among the most influential books ever written, for it was the work that introduced the eight parts of speech to the world. Before Dionysius' time, the classification of most words was up in the air. Aristotle and his successor spoke of nouns, verbs, and everything else; various more detailed systems of classification were proposed without catching on. Dionysius' swept away the competition. His book became a standard textbook for centuries. His system was adopted by Syrian, Armenian, and Roman grammarians. Via the last, especially Donatus and Priscian, his influence pervades the grammars of modern European languages.

In its surviving form, Dionysius' work consists of twenty very brief chapters, most no more than a short paragraph in length. The first ten chapters deal with phonics, the relationships between the letters of the Greek alphabet and the sounds that they represent. Chapter eleven introduces the notion of the sentence and eight parts of speech: "A sentence (*logos*) is an arrangement (*synthesis*) of words in prose[13] expressing a thought complete in itself (*dianoian autotele*). There are eight parts of speech: noun, verb, participle, article, pronoun, preposition, adverb, conjunction." To a modern reader, Dionysius' list has several striking peculiarities. He classifies adjectives as a subspecies of noun; articles and participles are categorized as separate parts of speech. What we now call interjections are viewed as adverbs. Nevertheless, his classification remains readily intelligible. It could be applied without revision to modern European languages, including English. The modern, canonical list involves relatively minor adjustments.

The remaining chapters in Dionysius' book give examples of each part of speech in order with some further subdivisions—e.g., the distinction between common and proper nouns. When he comes to verbs, Dionysius devotes an extra chapter to an overview of their morphology, which is very complicated in Greek.

Dionysius' grammar was followed by more comprehensive works on grammar. Those by Apollonius Dyscolus ("Apollonius the Irritable") who wrote in the second century A.D. were most highly regarded, but they followed the lines laid down by Dionysius.

Dionysius' achievement was the creation of a basic taxonomy of language, which has yet to be replaced or improved in any major way.[14] In turn, the mastery of this taxonomy became the first step in a liberal arts education. Thousands of years passed before anyone raised the question of whether this ability was worth cultivating. Intellectuals work with words. Questioning the value of basic grammar is like asking whether farmers should know the names of their crops and animals.

Dionysius' doctrine of the eight parts of speech was adopted by Roman grammarians. The Latin counterpart of Dionysius Thrax was Aelius Donatus, who flourished in Rome around A.D. 350. His pupils included St. Jerome, famous for translating the Bible into Latin. Donatus published literary commentaries, of which excerpts survive, and a two-part Latin grammar. The second part is a brief definition of the eight parts of speech with the formal title *Donati de Partibus Orationis Ars Minor* ("Donatus' Lesser Study Concerning the Parts of Speech"). It is in the form of a catechism:

> How many parts of speech are there?
> Eight.
> What are they?
> Noun, pronoun, verb, adverb, participle, conjunction, preposition, interjection.
> What is a noun?
> A part of speech with a case ending and signifying a person or thing specifically or generally.

As this quotation shows, articles—which Latin lacks—have been dropped, and interjections have been elevated from a subspecies of adverb to their own part of speech. The only difference between Donatus' list and the modern version is that he continues to include nouns and adjectives in the same group while putting participles into one of their own. Participles were later classified as forms of verbs.

Shortly before the fall of Rome, in the fifth century A.D., a scholar named Priscian produced a more comprehensive Latin grammar, inspired by the Greek grammatical studies of Apollonius Dyscolus. Priscian went beyond Donatus in various ways, including the extensive use of quotations from both Greek and Latin authors to illustrate his points. Priscian's quotation of classical sources shows how the rules of grammar were meant to be illustrated in education, viz., as embodied in classical literary works.

The books of Donatus and Priscian became the foundations of the study of grammar, and thus of the entire liberal arts curriculum, in the middle ages. Although Priscian was the great authority on grammar, Donatus' brief *de Partibus* was the most influential textbook. It was such a standard for so long that the term *donatist* or its equivalent came to denote a beginner in any field in several different languages. The study of grammar, however, eventually fell on hard times. As we shall now see, there are striking similarities between the educational scene at the present time and an earlier period in which instruction in grammar was devalued.

Notes

1. The Sanskrit alphabet, which is thought to have been derived from a Semitic script around 500 B.C., is more accurate phonetically than the Greek, but it is quite a bit harder to learn. What makes it difficult is that whenever vowels occur in the middle of words, they are indicated not by their own signs but by diacritical marks attached to the preceding consonant. The effect is that of a syllabary with several hundred different signs.

2. Powell, 20–21.

3. The uniqueness of the Greek literary achievements is widely recognized—e.g., Kirk, G. S., *The Iliad: A Commentary* (Cambridge: Cambridge University Press, 1985), I.14: "Nothing remotely approaching the quality of Homeric poetry is known from any other oral tradition"; William H. McNeill, *The Shape of European History* (Oxford: Oxford University Press, 1974), p. 56: "When all appropriate reservations have been made, there remains a special awe and reverence for what the Athenians and a few other Greeks accomplished. Who can compare with Herodotus and Thucydides among early writers of history? Or who can match Plato and Aristotle among philosophers? What literature excels Homer, Aeschylus, Sophocles, and Euripides?"

4. Perhaps because the oral nature of Homer's poems was first demonstrated by an American, Milman Parry, American classicists stress Homer's orality. German classicists are more likely to focus on the role that writing may have played in the final product—e.g. Joachim Latacz, *Homer, His Art and His World* (Ann Arbor: University of Michigan Press, 1996). See also Irene J. F. De Jong, "Homer as Literature: Some Current Areas of Research" in *Homeric Questions,* ed. J. P. Crielaard (Amsterdam: J. C. Gieben, 1995), 132.

5. It must be noted that a number of professional classicists are likely to take exception to this conclusion. An alternative view, finely presented in Kevin Robb's *Literacy and Paideia in Ancient Greece* (Oxford: Oxford University Press, 1994), is that literacy played only a marginal role in Greek culture until the late classical period. Briefly stated, my position is that the Robb camp gives too little weight to the evidence of widespread literacy in earlier Greece and leaves the cultural revolution of the archaic period without a plausible explanation. A clear example of the former tendency is Robb's dismissal of the fact preserved by Herodotus (6.27) that in 494 B.C. 119 boys, who were "studying their letters," were killed on the island of Chios when the roof of their school collapsed. Robb claims (p. 208) that Chios was "extraordinary," but his only evidence is that it was the location of readings of Homer in Hellenistic times. I am not suggesting that

the Greeks achieved anything like universal literacy, but I hold that writing in the hands of a few people in a number of critical enterprises, starting with literature, plausibly accounts for the otherwise mysterious dynamism that characterized the Greeks concurrently with the early spread of the use of the alphabet.

6. The primary source for this assertion is Stobaeus (fifth century A.D.), a Greek anthologist (2.31.27): "Crantor [a prominent member of the Academy] used to say that no one could be initiated into the Greater Mysteries before the Lesser Mysteries nor attain philosophy without laboring in the 'rounded' studies." Cp. Stobaeus, 2.31.22, 28, 11, and Diogenes Laertes (third century A.D.), 4.10.

7. The equivalence of the liberal arts with the "rounded education" is mentioned by Seneca (first century A.D.), *Epistles*, 88.23.

8. See the website of the Association of Graduate Liberal Studies Programs (AGLSP). A typical program, the one at North Central College (Naperville, Illinois), is directed by Dr. Richard Guzman, the president of the AGLSP. North Central's catalog description embodies the new concept of liberal studies nicely: "Central to (the) program is the belief that the word's growing complexity will continue to require specialization, but that specialization must be balanced by broader visions and wider perspectives. Business and technical professionals, teachers, community activists and persons in many other fields will gain the ability to make connections between separate disciplines, between life and learning, thought and action. . . . As knowledge from the arts, sciences, and humanities fuse [*sic*] with the concerns for ethics and leadership, students gain insights that not only fulfill them personally, but also lead to better ways of solving problems and dealing with conflict." *www.noctrl.edu/grad_catalog_2000/master_of_arts_degree_in_liberal_studies. shtml*, April 22, 2003.

9. Isocrates *Antidosis*, 267.

10. Seneca takes an interesting swipe at the philosophical treatment of grammar and mathematics: "I am speaking of the liberal arts, but how useless and impractical so much of our philosophy has become! Our philosophers study syllabification and definitions of conjunctions and prepositions, envying grammarians and geometers!"

11. Barrow, 17.

12. Gibb, 54.

13. Ancient commentators were puzzled by the limitation of the definition to prose but explained that poetry was characterized by ellipses and other embellishments that obscured the characteristics of a sentence. Some manuscripts have "in prose or poetry," which makes better sense, since Dionysius' first sentence defines grammar as "a study of things said by poets and prose-writers."

14. Contemporary linguists sometimes assert that the eight parts of speech are obsolete, but they are still used in dictionaries; cp. the tenth edition of the *Merriam-Webster Collegiate Dictionary*, 2001, p. 13a ("Function Labels"). Materials

produced by the British government for its national literacy strategy list the eight parts of speech as verb, adverb, preposition, conjunction, noun, pronoun, adjective, and determiner. The twentieth-century innovation in this list is the separation of determiners and adjectives, and people who speak of the obsolescence of the eight parts usually have determiners in mind. The distinction between determiners and adjectives, however, is not as clear as the distinctions among the other parts of speech. For example, the Merriam-Webster dictionary defines the term "determiner" as denoting articles, possessives, demonstratives, and quantifiers. In the individual articles for the relevant words, however, the part of speech is listed as "adjective," cp. *my, this, that, one, several, many,* and so forth. Articles (*the* and *a[n]*) are described as "function words."

Chapter Three

We've Passed This Way Before

Strangely Enough, the Rise of the University Spells the Decline of Grammar

Throughout the development of western civilization, beginning in the Hellenistic period, grammar has normally been viewed as the essential academic discipline on which all the others are based. The fact that so many modern teachers dispute the foundational importance of grammar is historically significant. For better or worse, it is something that sets our era apart from most previous ones.

Most, but not all. The twentieth century was the not the first period in which the study of grammar was relegated to the margins. The same thing happened in a previous era whose intellectual culture bears a number of striking resemblances to our own. I am speaking of the late middle ages, approximately A.D. 1100–1400. The intellectual style prevalent in Europe then became known as "scholasticism." Its successor was "humanism," the term used to designate the educational values that achieved dominance during the European Renaissance of the fifteenth and sixteenth centuries.

For most people, the Renaissance is epitomized by great works of art whose capacity to uplift and entertain has faded only slightly with the passage of time. Geographically and chronologically, its extent can be summarized by Botticelli's *Birth of Venus* in late fifteenth-century Italy and the plays of Shakespeare in early seventeenth-century England. Such is the legacy of the "humanists." If the impressions that I grew up with are typical, then most people think of these cultural milestones as representing the culmination of a long, slow but straight

43

ascent from the dark ages following the fall of Rome. In fact, there were some interesting twists and turns along the way, and grammar played a pivotal role.

German invaders dethroned the last Roman emperor in A.D. 476. This event was not, however, followed by the appearance of German authors emulating Greek and Roman literary achievements. In captivity, Rome did not captivate her fierce victor. The German rulers had a limited appreciation of the value of classical culture. The most famous case in point is that of Boethius, a great scholar who flourished briefly in the court of Theodoric the Great, the German king of Italy at the end of the fifth century. Boethius was eventually convicted of treason on dubious grounds and executed. At approximately the same time, the other leading scholar of the age, Cassiodorus, retired from government service and founded a monastery, where he and his monks devoted themselves to the study and preservation of ancient learning. Cassiodorus set the pattern for those wishing to preserve classical culture. His writings include an essay on the seven liberal arts, which together with Capella's volume was instrumental in perpetuating that tradition.

For the next three centuries, monasteries like Cassiodorus' were the leading institutions of learning and education in the western world. As a general rule, the only individuals to receive a higher education were life-long monks. Their education was based on the seven liberal arts and belief in Christianity. The goal of a monk's training was to preserve knowledge of ancient texts, especially the Bible, and the writings of the fathers of the church. It was assumed that these texts contained the correct answers to all the important questions. There was no market for intellectual originality.

After Rome's collapse, the first European monarch to become an effective patron of learning was Charlemagne, who founded the Holy Roman Empire by subjugating large portions of Germany, France, and Italy at the end of the eighth century. Charlemagne fostered the growth of education, supporting the work of scholars at his court in Aachen, encouraging scholarship in monasteries, and commanding the establishment of a school in the cathedrals in his realm. His initiatives led to an era of educational progress now called the "Carolingian Renaissance." Carolingian scholars devised a more attractive system of writing, Carolingian minuscules, from which modern typefaces descend. The Carolingian curriculum consisted of the seven liberal arts, with a heavy emphasis on memorization. A Carolingian music teacher, Guido d'Arezzo, invented the mnemonic musical scale, "do, re, mi."[1] Charlemagne himself was a champion of grammar, and the Carolingian curriculum emphasized correct and eloquent letter writing, the *ars dictaminis*, or "composition," as we would call it. This continued to be emphasized in Italian schools, even when interest waned elsewhere, and helped make Italy a leader of the later humanist movement.

For several centuries, medieval knights were invincible in war and thus had a considerable impact on European history. First, they accounted for Charlemagne's rise. Then, as their numbers grew, the security that they provided against disruptions, such as raids by Vikings, in combination with improved agricultural technology, fostered a period of economic growth in northwestern Europe that lasted from the eleventh century into the thirteenth.[2]

We have these medieval boom times to thank for modern universities. In the twelfth century, in the midst of increased trade, travel, and personal affluence, young scholars became a common sight as they traveled from town to town to study under the guidance of famous masters. Inevitably, some cities attracted more masters and scholars than others. Early on, Paris emerged as Europe's educational capital, but there were many other important venues. Universities began when groups of masters or students were given the legal status of guilds or corporations by the cities in which they resided. In its origin, the term "university" was roughly synonymous with "union": it referred simply to the integration into one group of an entire body of students or teachers. Between the latter half of the twelfth century and 1500, at least seventy-nine universities were founded in Europe, forty-nine of which survived into the twentieth century.[3] The rapid growth of universities is the first of several striking similarities between the late middle ages and the present era.

The Carolingian curriculum was founded on the painstaking study of the liberal arts. Old texts were read with punctilious care. Every word was parsed and scanned. The goal of composition was to write with the finesse of the classical masters no matter how long that might take. In the hustle and bustle of the twelfth century, however, with masters and universities competing for students and prestige, something flashier was needed, and it was found. The activity that came to typify the medieval universities and was the defining characteristic of scholasticism was the "disputation." This was a public event in which a master or a student defended a thesis against a series of negative arguments or provided a full set of affirmative and negative arguments himself.

The individual most responsible for popularizing the disputation was Peter Abelard, a brilliant, rebellious logician. His original analyses of theological issues kept him in constant conflict with established masters and church authorities and drew large crowds to his lectures at Mont Sainte-Genevieve outside Paris.

Abelard's great contribution was demonstrating that the revered authorities of the past disagree on numerous issues and are sometimes internally inconsistent. Hence, no matter how humble one may be, it is impossible simply to defer to authority on all issues. One must use logical analysis to get to the truth. Abelard's best-known work, *Sic et Non* ("Yes and No"; more literally "So and Not So"), is a collection of contradictory, though authoritative, opinions on 156 different propositions—e.g., that faith is based on reason, that nothing happens contrary to God's will, that Christians may not kill for any reason. In a preface, he gives logical rules for the resolution of contradictions. The enthusiasm roused by Abelard's approach is easier to understand when one considers its novelty at the time. For centuries, intellectuals had been trained simply to acquiesce to the authorities on all interesting questions. Now they could think for themselves.

Medieval disputants relied heavily on Aristotle's treatises on logic of which six, known collectively as the *Organum* ("The Instrument"), were ultimately recovered. Boethius had hoped to translate all of them into Latin but had finished only the first two when King Theodoric intervened. In the late twelfth and thirteenth century, the rest of the *Organum* was becoming available, translated from the Arabic and then directly from the Greek. The popularity of the disputation was thus enhanced by its utilization of the latest in ancient scholarship.

On the negative side, the popularity and prestige of the disputation was so great that other academic subjects were neglected. As in the twentieth century, philosophy's broad, traditional questions—e.g., how to lead a good life—tended to be disregarded as intellectually amateurish. Students were encouraged to engage in dialectics, or what we would call "critical thinking," without necessarily having mastered any other subject or discipline. By 1215, classical literature was completely absent from Paris's liberal arts curriculum: no poetry, no history, no rhetoric, no ethics—just logic.[4] Since grammar's traditional role was to enable students to understand the now-neglected classics, its prestige also declined sharply.

Two other factors hastened grammar's demise, and both have twentieth-century counterparts. The first stemmed from the growing practical importance of spoken Latin in the universities. As famous universities attracted more foreign students, an ever-higher value was placed on fluency in the international language. The need to be fluent in spoken Latin was also increased by the importance of shining in oral disputations. Scant attention was paid to fine points of grammar. Latin pedagogy became unabashedly pragmatic. Amusing examples of the kind of practical Latin that was valued are preserved in a fifteenth-century manual from Saxony, which contained "expressions frequently used by students" (*sermones qui a clericis sepius proferuntur*). These include excuses for being late for class: e.g., "I have been entertaining guests," (*ego propinavi hospitibus*); "I had a headache" (*dolorem capitis passus eram*); "My father made me water the horse" (*ex iussu patris mei adaquavi equum*).[5] Whereas Priscian's works were full of quotations from classical sources, the standard advanced Latin textbook of the late middle ages, Alexander's *Doctrinale*, emphasized Greek and Hebrew loan words that were used in theological and philosophical disputations. It had something of the character of a foreign language manual for a particular trade or business.

This contrast has exact parallels in contemporary classroom practice. The standard textbook in the late fifties and sixties in Latin, by Frederick Wheelock, published in 1956, illustrates Latin with literary aphorisms from the outset—e.g., "Avarice is never free of penalties"; "He gives twice who gives quickly." The textbook published by Oxford in 1987 is typical of the more recent approach. It introduces students to Latin with sentences like, "This boy is Quintus. Quintus is a Roman boy. Quintus lives in Apulia. Apulia is in Italy." The same tendency is even more pronounced in the study of modern languages. Now, as then, communication is in; grammar and eloquence are out.

Another parallel has to do with the last treatise in the *Organum* to be rediscovered in the West, *Posterior Analytics*. This was translated directly from the Greek by a certain James of Venice early in the twelfth century.[6] In *Posterior Analytics*, Aristotle lays down the ground rules for the establishment of scientific knowledge (*episteme*) using mathematics and geometry as models. Scientific propositions must be deduced with logical certainty from indubitable axioms or first principles and apply without exception to all the particulars comprehended by the definitions of its terms. A true science is ipso facto universal.

Under the influence of *Posterior Analytics*, scholars in various fields sought to put their disciplines on a more scientific footing. Among those influenced were grammarians, who attempted to formulate grammatical definitions that could meet this more rigorous standard.[7] Since (as we have seen) the traditional eight parts of speech do not capture all the differences in the ways that words are used, they were further subdivided into various "modes of signifying," which greatly complicated the traditional taxonomy. From this terminology, advocates of the new scientific grammar were known as "modistae." The modistae believed that the grammatical qualities that they identified in Latin sentences had exact counterparts in external reality. In their minds, they were striving to describe the rules of a universal grammar, not those of a particular language. Grammar as they practiced it was a science aimed at discovering absolute truths, not a practical discipline by which people might learn to read with comprehension and speak and write well. Hence, their discipline became known as "speculative grammar."

Medieval speculative grammar is identical in its aspirations to one of the twentieth century's most famous intellectual projects, transformational grammar, which burst on the scene with the publication of

Noam Chomsky's *Syntactic Structures* in 1957 and continues to be a major academic enterprise. Then, as now, the emergence of speculative grammar diminished the prestige of traditional grammar, even though the two enterprises are logically quite distinct.

Though scholasticism was dominant in the twelfth century, a few schools—e.g., those at Orleans and Chartes—continued to emphasize traditional, practical grammar and the close study of classical literature, and champions of such curricula were critical of scholasticism from the outset. The most articulate was John of Salisbury, a British scholar, who studied under Abelard and two successors at Mont Sainte-Genevieve in Paris. His four-volume work on education, *The Metalogicon,* is considered to be the best first-hand account of education in the twelfth century.

John was duly impressed by Abelard's brilliance but less smitten by the teachings of two successors, Alberic and Robert of Melun. In John's descriptions, these scholars sound like forerunners of the postmodernists. Alberic, we are told, could find contradictions in any position—"knots in bullrushes"—while Robert could make any proposition sound plausible. In fact, Robert would never finish a lecture without proving the opposite of his original thesis. John's conclusion is that both men could have become great intellectuals "had they but possessed a broad foundation of literary learning, and kept to the footsteps of their predecessors as much as they took delight in their own inventions."[8]

From Paris, John migrated to the cathedral school at Chartes, a bastion of traditionalism. Its curriculum reflected the opinions of its great chancellor, Bernard of Chartes. In describing Bernard's pedagogy, John quotes Quintilian's advice that "the teacher of grammar should, in lecturing, take care of such details as to have his students analyze verses into their parts of speech, and point out the nature of the metrical feet which are to be noted in poems. He should, furthermore, indicate and condemn whatever is barbarous, incongruous, or otherwise against the rules of composition."[9] Bernard did all this and more—e.g., assigning his students daily compositions in poetry or prose modeled on classical authors. John studied grammar in Chartes for three years under William of Conches and Richard the Bishop, less renowned masters who adhered to Bernard's methods. John says that he learned much in this way and would never regret the time spent there. Times, however, were changing:

> Later, when popular opinion veered away from the truth, when men preferred to seem, rather than to be, philosophers, and when professors of the arts were promising to impart the whole of philosophy in less than three or even two years, William and Richard were overwhelmed by the onslaught of the ignorant mob, and retired. Since then, less time and attention have been given to the study of

grammar. As a result, we find men who profess all the arts, liberal and mechanical, but who are ignorant of this very first one, without which it is futile to go on to attempt the others.[10]

After further travels, John returned to Mont Sainte-Genevieve to visit his old comrades, who were still studying dialectics:

> I found them just as, and where, they were when I had left them. They did not seem to have progressed as much as a hand's span. Not a single tiny proposition had they added toward the solution of the old problems. They themselves remained involved in and occupied with the same questions whereby they used to stir their students. They had changed in but one regard: they had unlearned moderation: they no longer knew restraint. . . . I was accordingly convinced by experience of something which can easily be inferred by reason: that just as dialectic expedites other studies, so, if left alone by itself, it lies powerless and sterile.[11]

As Isocrates would have said, John's friends had lingered too long in the elementary discipline of logic and ended up as "mere skeletons, stranded on the subtleties of the ancient sophists."

The thirteenth century provides another illuminating example of such criticism, a satirical allegory in French, "The Battle of the Seven Arts," written in 1259 by Henri d'Andeli, a scholar from Rouen. This work is sometimes mentioned as an early example of the tension between champions of ancient and modern authors, respectively, an earlier version of Swift's *Battle of the Books,* but d'Andeli actually addresses a more complex issue. The theme of his poem, announced in the first lines, is that there is destructive hostility between the advocates of different disciplines, Logic at Paris versus Grammar and the "authors"—i.e., literature—at Orleans. Each party despises the other, but they do so on disciplinary, not chronological, grounds. On the one hand, the "authors" championed by Orleans include both ancients and moderns, poets and rhetoricians, bound together by their devotion to eloquence, the artistic use of language. The logicians, on the other hand, represent a modern approach to education but do not disdain the ancients as such. Aristotle is their greatest champion and Plato also fights on their side, as do the ancient authorities of other sciences.

Since Logic has won over most of the students, Grammar is angry and marches on Paris. In the ensuing battle, each side is deficient in its own ways. The grammarians, we are told, could have defended themselves except that their fortresses were "stocked with fables" (*garnis de fables*). At one juncture, Logic sends one of her pupils out to negotiate a truce with Grammar, but not understanding syntax, he is unable to get to the point (*venir a chef*) and returns in shame.

> Logic comforted him,
>
> Carried him to her high tower,
>
> And tried to make him fly
>
> Before he was able to walk.[12]

Logic was dominant in the schools and is therefore depicted as winning d'Andeli's allegorical battle. D'Andeli laments the resulting situation, not because he thinks that Grammar and the authors should reign supreme by themselves. His theme is the same as John's. Logic needs to be grounded in the preliminary study of grammar and literature.

> Sirs, the times are given to emptiness;
>
> Soon they will go entirely to naught.
>
> For thirty years this will continue,
>
> Until a new generation will arise,
>
> Who will go back to Grammar,
>
> Just as it was the fashion
>
> When Henri d'Andeli was born,
>
> Who gives it us as his opinion
>
> That one should destroy the glib student
>
> Who cannot construe his lesson;
>
> For in every science that "master" is a mere child[13]
>
> Who has not mastered his parts of speech.[14]

The Return of the Humanities

D'Andeli was correct in prophesying the return of grammar but overly optimistic in his time frame. It was nearly a hundred years, rather than merely thirty, before the reaction against scholasticism took shape in the form of "humanism."

Until recently, scholars thought that the distinctive characteristic of the humanist movement was a philosophical focus on human nature in contrast with the theological concerns of the middle ages. This view, however, has been overturned largely through the work of one man, Paul Oskar Kristeller, whose careful analysis of primary sources has brought to light a different picture. Kristeller has shown that the Renaissance "humanists" did not subscribe to any revolutionary philosophical doctrines. What distinguished them was their pursuit of a different array of intellectual interests than those of the scholastics. The humanists sought specifically to revive the studies of grammar, rhetoric, poetry, history, and moral philosophy.

The movement first took shape in the mid-fourteenth century in the circle of poet and scholar Francesco Petrarch. The humanists' own phrase for their intellectual interests, *studia humanitatis,* was taken from a speech by Cicero, "For the poet Archias," which does much to explain the spirit of the movement.[15] Cicero's defendant, Archias, was a poet from Antioch who had resided in Rome for many years, earning patronage through his verse. Enemies had brought him to trial claiming that he had never become a citizen and should be expelled from the city. Cicero provided the defense, answering the technical charges but also taking advantage of the situation to share his views on the value of studying literature.

Cicero's defense is impassioned and ultimately subjective. He says that he would not have the energy to pursue his strenuous political career if he could not refresh himself with literary studies and that they give him inspirational examples of human greatness. Yet, he says, even supposing that pleasure is the only purpose of literary studies, they should still be viewed as enlightened and noble:

> Other diversions do not belong to all times, all ages, all places. Literary studies sharpen the minds of youth, entertain the elderly, glorify successes, offer refuge and comfort in adversity, give delight at home, are no impediment in society, stay with us through sleepless nights, on foreign journeys, in the lonely countryside.[16]

Here Cicero is tackling a problem that bedevils any defense of literary studies: There is no logically compelling way to demonstrate their value. None of society's essential jobs requires the knowledge of literary classics. One can only appeal, as Cicero does, to shared, subjective experience. Literary studies, he says, are profoundly enjoyable and, unlike most other pleasures, we never seem to outgrow or regret them. On the contrary, enjoying a literary classic leaves us with the conviction that we have done something good for our mind or spirit, even though we cannot say precisely what it is. At the heart of the humanist movement was the belief that education had no higher goal than to foster this edifying pleasure.

In his own defense of literary studies, Petrarch emphasizes not only the pleasure obtained from the words of others but also the emotional healing achieved through eloquent self-expression:

> How delightful is it at times to repeat the writings of others or my own, and to feel through such reading how I am actually freed from the burden of the weightiest and most bitter troubles! In this I am sometimes aided more by my own words, in that they are more suited to my languishing sickness, for they are words which have been applied by the knowledgeable hand of a doctor who was languishing himself and could feel where the pain was.[17]

Petrarch's opinions on dealing with grief are not to be taken lightly. He lived through the horrible years of the Black Death (1348–50), which claimed the lives of his beloved Laura and a veritable legion of other friends and acquaintances. An excerpt from a letter to a friend after the first year of the plague conveys a sense of what he was going through:

> We used to be a crowd. Now we are almost alone. We have to form new friendships. But where, and for what reason, since the whole race of men is nearly extinct, and the end of the world, I hope, is near. We are alone brother, we are—why hide it—truly alone.[18]

To enjoy great literature, one must understand it. To apply the balm of self-expression to internal wounds, one must first know the proper use of words. Hence, for both reasons, the humanists' most urgent task was to reform the teaching of Latin grammar. Alexander's *Doctrinale*, which was responsible for legitimizing nonclassical, conversational Latin, needed to be superseded, and instruction in grammar had to be purged of the theoretical speculations of the modistae.

The Italian humanist who provided the greatest boost to the reform of grammatical instruction throughout Europe was Petrarch's fellow Italian, Lorenzo Valla. A brilliant Latinist, Valla gained fame by debunking the "Donation of Constantine," a supposed grant of territory by the emperor to the Pope, through an analysis of its nonclassical style. A subsequent essay urging a return to classical usages, *De Linguae Latinae Elegantia* ("On the elegance of the Latin language"), written around 1440 and first printed in 1471, became one of the most influential works of the age.

In due course, new humanist Latin grammars modeled on Donatus and Priscian appeared throughout Europe. Though inspired by the works of Latin authors, they went beyond these models and the later scholastic textbooks by providing glosses and translations of grammatical terms and paradigms into vernacular languages. Donatus, of course, had written entirely in Latin. The inclusion of vernacular explanations was a wonderful expression of the humanist opposition to scholastic obscurantism. To revive the ability to read classical texts with appreciation, more was required than "receptive competence." Students were to be given explanations of grammatical rules in terms that they could fully understand.

While the inclusion of vernacular explanations served this purpose, it had the additional and possibly unintended benefit of inaugurating the conscious grammatical analysis of vernacular languages. That in turn helped literary artists achieve great new heights in those languages. One might think that the activities of the champions of classical Latin would have retarded the development of vernacular literature, but exactly the opposite occurred. The project of appreciating classical Latin was intertwined with that of fostering vernacular eloquence from the outset. In Italy, where an appreciation of classical Latin never really died, the flowering of vernacular literature preceded and helped to motivate the humanist reforms, as the works of Dante, Boccaccio, and Petrarch himself show. Elsewhere in Europe, the appearance of a new humanistic grammar of Latin, followed by a vernacular counterpart, was the prelude to, or a concomitant of, the rise of vernacular literatures.[19] Grammar's dual role, preserving or reviving the appreciation of literary classics and creating new eloquence, was never illustrated more dramatically.

The Educational Reform That Gave Us Shakespeare

The intellectual chiefly responsible for introducing humanism to England was Desiderius Erasmus. One of his particular concerns was reforming instruction in grammar, especially by eliminating the modistae's confusing ideas. In Erasmus' best-known work, *The Praise of Folly*, the speaker, Folly personified, devotes a long passage to the fatuity of then-modern grammarians:

> No one could be more wretched, more miserable, more despised by the gods than they would be if I did not soften the hard lot of this most pitiful profession with a certain kind of sweet madness. . . . What makes them [happy] is a certain strange conviction they harbor about their learning. Though in fact most of them pound nothing but sheer nonsense into the boys' heads, still, by all the gods! how they look down their noses even at Palaemon[20] or Donatus! . . . I know a certain polymath, who knows Greek, Latin, mathematics, philosophy, and medicine . . . already in his sixties, who has abandoned everything else and for more than twenty years has been tormenting himself and beating out his brains about grammar. He would consider himself perfectly happy if he could live long enough to determine once and for all how the eight parts of speech can be distinguished from each other—something which up to now no one has done to perfection in either Greek or Latin. . . . For this reason, though there are almost as many grammars as grammarians, . . . he never passes over a single one, no matter how barbarously or wretchedly written.[21]

As is clear from his other works, Erasmus believed that young students needed to be trained in elementary grammar in the tradition of Dionysius and Donatus. This was to provide a foundation for the study of classical works of literature, selected for their aesthetic appeal, and for the cultivation of the students' own eloquence. What drew Erasmus' scorn was the transformation of grammar by the modistae into an impractical, esoteric, speculative discipline on which nitpicking old scholars wasted their powers.

Erasmus visited England early in the reign of King Henry VIII, spreading the gospel of humanism in elite circles. *The Praise of Folly* is dedicated to Thomas More. Another one of Erasmus' influential British friends was John Colet, who endowed and re-established one of London's leading cathedral schools, St. Paul's, in 1509. St. Paul's became the first of the Renaissance grammar schools in England. Like Chartes under Bernard, it focused on the study of classical literature based on a firm foundation of grammar. Colet appointed classical scholar William Lily as the first high master of St. Paul's School. Among Lily's responsibilities was the compilation of a grammar to be used by his students. He composed a short work on the eight parts of speech, which was amended by Erasmus and published throughout Europe under the latter's name. In the 1540s, Lily's treatise on the parts of speech was combined with a work on morphology by Colet and published with a decree by Henry VIII prescribing its exclusive use in all British schools. A definitive edition appeared in 1574, after which no further changes were made.[22]

A letter to the reader in a 1544 version of Lily's grammar explains the rationale behind King Henry's decree. The influence of Erasmus' criticism of speculative grammar is obvious:

> His majesty considering the great encumbrance and confusion of the young and tender wits, by reason of the diversity of grammar rules and teachings (for heretofore every master had his grammar, and every school diverse teachings, and changing of masters and schools did many times utterly dull and undo good wits) hath appointed certain learned men meet for such a purpose, to compile one brief, plain, and uniform grammar, which only (all others set apart) for the more speediness, and less trouble of young wits, his highness hath commanded all schoolmasters and teachers of grammar within this his realm, and other his dominions, to teach their scholars.[23]

Lily's grammar was designed to enable students to read classical Latin literature. It is a straightforward exposition of Latin morphology and syntax based on the eight parts of speech. Students were required to memorize Latin's complicated system of inflectional endings by reciting paradigms. As in other humanistic grammars, all the features of Latin were explained by giving their vernacular—viz., English—equivalents. Thus students were exposed to the fact that sentences in English also had subjects consisting of nouns and pronouns and that

English verbs also had different forms expressing various tenses, moods, and voices. They learned about main clauses and main verbs:

> Whan an englishe [sentence] is given to be made in latine, looke out the principall verbe. If there bee more verbes than one in a sentence, the firste is the principall verbe, except it be the infinitive mode, or have before it a relative: as *that, whom, which:* or a conjunctrion: as *Ut, that; Cum, whan; Si, if:* or suche others.[24]

As my students' struggles with the Declaration of Independence show, this is also a helpful piece of advice for reading English with comprehension. Unlike them, Lily's students were trained to think about English, as well as Latin, grammatically.

The promulgation of "one brief, plain, uniform grammar" in British schools occurred on the eve of the English literary Renaissance. From Chaucer's death in 1400 to the mid-sixteenth century, England did not produce any literary artists of lasting fame. Then the students who had been raised on Lily's grammar started coming of age: Edmund Spenser (1552–99), Francis Bacon (1561–1626), Christopher Marlowe (1564–93), John Ford (1568–1639), Ben Jonson (1572–1637), and, of course, William Shakespeare (1564–1616).

In a posthumous poetic tribute,[25] Ben Jonson wrote that Shakespeare had "small Latin, less Greek." This frequently quoted line is extremely misleading when viewed outside of its historical context. Though no documents survive to tell us with certainty where Shakespeare went to school, chronological considerations and references in his works have left scholars certain that he attended a grammar school shaped by the Erasmian reforms.[26] In all likelihood, it was the free grammar school at Stratford. If so, his teacher was Thomas Jenkins. All matters touching on Shakespeare's education have been closely studied, and it appears that the curriculum in Jenkins's own grammar school was modeled on St. Paul's.[27] If so, there is a direct thread connecting Shakespeare to the reforms of Erasmus and Colet.

In any event, barring extraordinary circumstances, for which there is no evidence, Shakespeare's education consisted of grounding in Lily's grammar followed by the reading of classical Latin authors and, if he stayed in school long enough, a smattering of Greek. Because of the centrality of classical Greek and Latin in education, the standards of Ben Jonson were roughly the same as those of a professional classicist today. By such standards, I might say that some present-day Classics major had "small Latin, less Greek." That would mean that he or she had read excerpts of some major classical Latin texts and knew the rudiments of classical Greek. Of such a student, as of Shakespeare, it would be safe to assume an understanding of the material that is covered in Lily's grammar.

In fact, the assumption that Shakespeare studied Lily's grammar is confirmed by his allusion to it. In *Merry Wives of Windsor* (IV.1), a fatuous parson quizzes a schoolboy on the declension of *hic* (this), Latin's most irregular adjective, which is constantly employed in Lily to indicate the case, number, and gender of various nouns. The boy does well until the parson asks him for the vocative case of *hic*. In fact, this form is nonexistent, because one does not use demonstratives in Latin or English to refer to the person being addressed: "O this man." When Shakespeare's schoolboy hesitates, the parson informs him that the vocative of *hic* is *caret*, which is an absurd thing to say. *Caret* just means "it is missing" and is used by Lily for theoretically possible forms that do not actually occur. In fact, the declension of *hic* is given at the beginning of Lily and Colet's *Short Introduction of Grammar* in terms that are echoed by Shakespeare:

> Nominativo: hic, haec, hoc
>
> Genitivo: huius
>
> Dativo: huic
>
> Accusat.: hunc, hanc, hoc
>
> Vocativo: caret[28]

It is an inside joke that clearly betrays Shakespeare's familiarity with Lily's grammar.

Even apart from direct allusions, anyone who has studied Latin grammar and applied its lessons to English recognizes a kindred spirit in Shakespeare. So many of his sentences are elaborate syntactic structures, complex but lucid. Consider, for example, the twenty-ninth Sonnet:

> When, in disgrace with fortune and men's eyes,
>
> I all alone beweep my outcaste state,
>
> And trouble deaf heaven with my bootless cries,
>
> And look upon myself, and curse my fate,
>
> Wishing me like to one more rich in hope,
>
> Featured like him, like him with friends possest,
>
> Desiring this man's art, and that man's scope,
>
> With what I most enjoy contented least;
>
> Yet in these thoughts myself almost despising,
>
> Haply I think on thee, and then my state,
>
> Like to the lark at break of day arising
>
> From sullen earth, sings hymns at heaven's gate;
>
> > For thy sweet love remembered such wealth brings
> >
> > That then I scorn to change my state with kings'.

The first complete sentence (through "think on thee") consists of seventy-five words tightly arranged into a dependent and main clause. The finite verb in the subordinate clause is quadruply compounded (beweep, trouble, look, curse) and is followed by four participles (wishing, desiring, contented, despising) that modify the subject, I—Latinate syntax that can be made to work in English if one is careful, as Shakespeare is, to make it clear on semantic grounds which substantive the participles modify. The participial phrases have their own complications. "Wishing," for example, is used as factitive verb with a direct object and three object complements (wishing me [1.] like one ... [2.] featured ... [3.] possest). After this prelude, the simplicity of the main clause, "haply I think on thee," has a wonderful impact. The final couplet contains a "result clause" of the kind that is a staple of classical Latin and a major topic in elementary Latin grammar ("such wealth ... that . . . I scorn ...").

According to Samuel Johnson, Shakespeare "had Latin enough to grammaticize his English."[29] Though it comes to the same thing, I would prefer to say that he had *grammar* enough to "grammaticize" his English. Understanding Latin has no bearing per se on one's ability to write English, but the grammatical foundation on which Latin study is based in the humanist approach is directly relevant. The grammatical concepts are the transportable elements, and they are what even students with "small Latin" acquire.[30]

I began this chapter by suggesting that there are a number of parallels between the era of medieval scholasticism and our own day. I will close by mentioning one more. The end of the scholasticism and the rise of humanism was accompanied by the development of modern printing. The obvious counterpart is the Internet, representing another quantum leap in the ease with which visual speech may be disseminated. Then, the rise of humanism led to an improvement in the quality as well as the quantity and accessibility of books. Now, conventional wisdom takes a pessimistic view of the effect of the Internet on our language. Decline is not inevitable, however. The fact that anyone can communicate effortlessly with thousands of people all over the world *could* lead to a renewed interest in eloquence. If a new generation of humanists comes along, it will have a glorious challenge.

The dark side of medieval scholasticism was the Inquisition. The Dominicans, who rose to prominence as scholars in the twelfth century and gave us Thomas Aquinas, one of the great minds of western civilization, were also responsible for Bernard Gui, the dark-hearted cleric familiar to many from *The Name of the Rose*. As the Inquisition suggests, problems in Scholasticism reflected intellectual hubris. The scholastics assumed that every intellectual endeavor worthy of the name was scientific in Aristotle's sense—i.e., like geometry, it consisted of a set of absolute truths derived by the universal laws of logic from axioms that could not be doubted because they were a priori truths or because they had been firmly established a posteriori by empirical observation. Scientific certainty is a noble aspiration, but it has a great and obvious limitation. In many areas of profound interest to human beings, there are no axioms, no first principles from which certain truths can be logically deduced. The scholastics evaded this inconvenient fact by disregarding some of these—literature, history, and ethics—and by presuming to have axiomatic knowledge in other areas that really were, and still are, anchored in mystery—meaning religion, of course, but also language. Humanism represented disillusionment with scientific thinking *as a panacea* and the consequent rediscovery of the uses of tradition and common sense.

Notes

1. Piltz, 21.
2. McNeill, 88.
3. Norton, 6.
4. Bursill-Hall, 24.
5. Haskins, 89–90.
6. Dod, 55.
7. Pinborg, 255.
8. John of Salisbury, II.10 (96).
9. John of Salisbury, I.24 (66).
10. John of Salisbury, I.24 (71).
11. John of Salisbury, II.10 (100).
12. Henri d'Andeli, 393–97.
13. "Mere child" is *gars* ("stripling") in the French.
14. d'Andeli, 450–61.
15. *Pro Archia*, 3: "I ask that in this case you grant me a favor, suitable for this defendant and not, I should hope, annoying to you: that you permit me . . . to speak rather freely about the studies of humanity and literature (*de studiis humanitatis ac litterarum*)." In Petrarch's day, many classical texts lay forgotten in monasteries. He himself rediscovered the *Pro Archia* in a monastery in Liege in 1344 and brought it to the attention of the educated world; cp. John E. Sandys, *Harvard Lectures on the Revival of Learning* (Boston: Harvard University Press, 1905), p. 16.
16. *Pro Archia*, 16 (my translation).
17. Rebhorn, 17.
18. Proctor, 28.

19. In Spain, Nebrija published *Introductiones Latinae* in 1481 and a vernacu-
    lar grammar, *Gramatica Castillana,* in 1492; cp. Padley 1985, 157–59. In
    France, Despauterius' *Rudimenta* appeared in 1514, a compilation of his
    grammatical writings in 1537; cp. Padley 1976, 19. Early vernacular French
    grammars include Jacques Dubois *In Linguam Gallicam Isogoge* 1531; cp.
    Padley 1985, 331. Melanchthon's humanist Latin grammar, *Grammatica
    Latina,* was published in 1525 in Germany; cp. Padley 1976, 21. Albertus'
    vernacular *Teutsch Grammatick* followed in 1573; cp. Padley 1985, 260.

20. Quintus Remmius Palaemon, a celebrated Roman grammarian of the first
    century A.D., Quintilian's teacher.

21. Erasmus, 1511, ff. 79–80.

22. Padley, 1985, 231–32.

23. Lily, 2.

24. Lily and Colet, 32.

25. "To the Memory of My Beloved, the Author Mr. William Shakespeare."

26. Baldwin, i.464.

27. Baldwin, i.418.

28. Lily and Colet. Several early pages, including the relevant one, are miss-
    ing from the 1549 edition reproduced by Scolar Press Limited. Appendix
    1, however, contains the equivalent pages from a 1557 edition. The par-
    adigm of *hic* occurs on the third page of the appendix. The original page
    bore the number 8.

29. Baldwin, ii.668.

30. The first grammar of vernacular English, William Bullokar's *Bref Grammar,*
    did not appear until 1586. It was based on Lily's grammar and its elucida-
    tions of grammatical concepts in English. Bullokar has been criticized for
    trying to force English into the mold of Latin, but his particular mistakes
    do not seem to justify the weight that has been given to the general charge
    of being too reliant on Latin. Arthur Padley, a leading authority on the his-
    tory of grammar until his death in 1986, described Bullokar's "major er-
    ror" as the attribution to English of Latin categories that are not "formally
    marked" in English. For example, Bullokar speaks of the noun subjects of
    sentences as being in the nominative case, as though the unitary words
    contained some case marking. He does not betray any "realization that sub-
    ject and object are indicated in English by position within the sentences."
    A more generous interpretation is that, since this realization is possessed
    intuitively by all English speakers, it was merely taken for granted by
    Bullokar. In any event, as Padley notes, Bullokar and other early vernac-
    ular grammarians did demonstrate that "English possesses exact analytical
    counterparts to the Latin morphological system." In other words, they
    showed that English, like Latin, has subjects, objects, indirect objects, ob-
    jects of prepositions, absolute phrases, verbs in the active and passive voices
    and perfect and imperfect tenses, finite verbs, participles, gerunds, and in-
    finitives, and so on. These benefits seem to outweigh a handful of errors
    in which the Latin model is overused.

Chapter Four

The War Against Grammar

Progressive Education

For two thousand years, no one in the western tradition challenged the notion that education should be based on the liberal arts, starting with grammar. In the late middle ages, logic achieved such prestige in higher education that grammar and rhetoric suffered de facto neglect, but they were still respected in theory. It was not until the beginning of the twentieth century in America that a full-fledged revolt against the liberal arts occurred. This happened under the banner of "progressive education," a pervasive movement in American education responsible for many things, both good and bad. Its bad effects result from carrying reactions against the liberal arts tradition to unjustified extremes. The elimination of formal instruction in grammar from the grade school curriculum is an example of such an extreme.

There have been two major currents in progressive education. They pertain to curricular content and pedagogical method, respectively. Both currents put progressives on a collision course with grammar.

Around the turn of the century, the number of students going to high school began to increase dramatically, from approximately 5 percent in 1890, to 10 percent in 1900, 14 percent in 1910, and 31 percent in 1920.[1] This historic change became the occasion of debates over the content of the curriculum. Previously, the K–12 curriculum was viewed as an narrow ladder leading to study at a college or a university and was based on the liberal arts. The constant features were the study of Latin, with emphasis on grammar, and of mathematics. The majority of students, however, never reached college. They dropped off the educational ladder after its first few rungs. The great increase in the numbers of such students naturally led educators to consider revising the curriculum to make it more directly beneficial for the majority of students and geared less to the preferences of college professors. They argued that students should receive training in specific vocations and for other practical challenges that they would face as adults in the nonacademic world.

Such was the basic impulse behind progressive education, which quickly became ascendant within the K–12 teaching profession—i.e., among K–12 teachers themselves and professors in schools of education. The history of Columbia's Teachers College, the cynosure of schools of education, shows how this happened. The Teachers College began humbly, as the Kitchen Garden Association, in 1880. Its purpose then was to help girls escape poverty by training them in cooking and domestic service. The Kitchen Garden Association, soon added courses for boys in the industrial arts and grew apace. Then, in a fateful move, it decided to focus on a different area of burgeoning demand: the preparation of primary and secondary school teachers. In this way, it gained a mission that combined the best of both worlds, practicality and intellectual prestige: vocational training for people whose vocation was academic. In 1892, it was given a permanent charter as the Teachers College, a new division of Columbia University. This set the pattern for schools of education such as are found in most universities today. It was not just another normal school where aspiring teachers acquired basic liberal arts competencies, but a professional school sponsoring research and offering advanced degrees in pedagogy. In all of this, it should not be lost sight of that the origin of modern schools of education was the desire to offer alternatives to training in the liberal arts for the benefit of students who were not going to go to college.[2]

Besides introducing practical subjects into the curriculum, progressive educators have always taken a dim view, methodologically, of "formalism" in teaching. This is an elusive concept, but I believe that it is best understood by reference to the distinction between determinate and reflective judgments introduced in Chapter One. *Formalism* means emphasis on determinate judgments. It trades in rules and definitions that are specified ahead of time and is based on the assumption that, for any question, there is one correct answer, which the teacher knows and the student must be trained to produce.

As rudimentary, practical subjects, the liberal arts have a natural affinity for formal modes of instruction. This is especially true of grammar. The point is not to reflect on the interesting behavior of words, but to learn basic rules and definitions—and to move on. Accordingly, in earlier eras, pedagogical methods in grammar and the other liberal arts were brutally simple. Students were given material to memorize and were beaten if they failed to do so. As an adult, the Roman poet Horace reports that he still remembers the verses taught to him by his grammar teacher, Orbilius *plagosus*—Orbilius "full of beatings" (*Epistles*, 2.1.70). John of Salisbury mentions "flogging" among the sound pedagogical methods employed by Bernard of Chartes, France's "greatest font of wisdom."[3] As we have seen, Donatus' grammar was cast in the form of a catechism, meant to be memorized. Even the long, advanced Latin grammar of the later middle ages, Alexander's *Doctrinale*, was written in meter to assist memorization.

There is something to be said for hard-nosed, formal instruction—for rote learning. Knowing specified rules and definitions gives students autonomy. When they are right, they are right. They do not have to rely on a teacher's subjective approval. Also, not every youth is crushed by intimidating pedagogy. Some flourish. Horace certainly did. Still, there is obviously more to an ideal education than "memorize this or else," and progressive educators have always been dedicated to explaining what that *more* is.

John Dewey is the great founding father of progressive education. Central to his writings is the conviction that there was too much formalism in the schools of his day,[4] and he was most probably right. The amount of factual information that grade school students early in the twentieth century were expected to know is incredible by contemporary standards. In geography, for example, students had to answer questions like the following in order to graduate from the *eighth grade* in Nebraska in 1921:

1. Name and locate the mountain systems of each continent and give the directions in which they extend.

2. Name four of the greatest wheat raising countries in the world.

3. Name three plains of South America and tell for what each is noted.

4. What are the principal occupations of the people of Australia?

5. Name two large rivers that flow into the Arctic Ocean; two that flow into the Atlantic Ocean, and two that flow into the Pacific Ocean.[5]

It is easy to understand how school systems producing tests like these gave rise to Dewey's critique, but it also important to note that his critique was not radical. He argued that educators should seek "a proper balance between the formal and informal,"[6] not the abolition of the former. This is a fact of critical importance in gaining a proper perspective on the chronic debate between progressives and traditionalists: there is no difference in principle between the reasonable representatives of these two seemingly hostile points of view. If Dewey had come along in the year 2003, he surely would have fought for more formal instruction in American schools; in 1921, E. D. Hirsch would have championed less emphasis on mere facts.

The goal of education can be broadly conceived as the development of the ability to make good judgments, both formal and informal, determinate and reflective. In most activities outside of school, determinate and reflective judgments are interwoven. Physicians have to make determinate diagnoses while also gaining their patients' trust in reflective conversations. Education, however, should focus on one kind of judgment at a time, since it is hard to teach different things simultaneously. Though they are both necessary and interdependent—like rest and exercise—determinate and reflective judgments must be fostered and evaluated in opposite ways. Determinate judgments rely on memorization. Repetition makes people better at them. They can be evaluated with relative ease through objective testing. In contrast, reflective judgments rely on interest. Repetition is deadly, as is the feeling that the teacher already knows the "right" answer. In fact, a student's reflective judgments are often better than the teacher's. Students should alternate between the exercise of reflective judgment, in evaluating literature for example, and the development of determinate judgment through the memorization of rules, definitions, and facts, while their teachers adjust their own behavior accordingly. The ideal approach to education is one that alternates in a rational way between progressive and traditional approaches.

In fact, the recognition of the contrasting character of determinate and reflective judgments and of the importance of each lies at the heart of a famous, early model of progressive education, that implemented by the public school system of Winnetka, Illinois, in 1919. The Winnetka curriculum was designed by Carleton Washburne on the basis of research done at San Francisco State Normal School, a center of educational reform during the First World War. Washburne began by dividing the curriculum between "the common essentials," such as the three Rs, and other subjects that gave each child a chance for "self-expression and the opportunity to contribute to the group something of his own special interests and abilities."[7] The common essentials were taught through self-instructional booklets. Students worked through these at their own pace, but they were not permitted to advance until they had demonstrated mastery of the material at each successive level. The student's choice lay between mastering the objective content of the common essentials booklets and being left behind. In other words, "memorize this or else."

The curriculum was considered successful, remaining in place for decades. The students' scores in reading, language, and arithmetic improved on standardized testing. Evaluators were inclined to believe that the curriculum was also good for student initiative and self-reliance, but they acknowledged that such traits could not be accurately measured.

Grammar was one of Winnetka's common essentials. In fact, the time devoted to it was increased over the years.[8] In other words, there was no intrinsic opposition between the goals of progressive education and formal instruction in grammar. As long as a balance between formal and informal subjects, recommended by Dewey, was the desideratum, common sense dictated that the foundational subjects like grammar and arithmetic would continue to be taught formally.

Problems stemmed from the institutionalizing of pedagogical research in schools of education. This created a market for new theories of education in the same way that the advanced study of literature has produced an endless stream of new interpretations of classical works. Inevitably, some scholars involved in such an enterprise carry their theories to extremes. In schools of education, extremists proposed that one could go further in minimizing attention to the liberal arts and reducing formal instruction than John Dewey ever dreamed.

The educational extremist who had the greatest influence on American education was William Kilpatrick. A charismatic lecturer, Kilpatrick burst on the educational scene with an influential essay in which he advocated a curriculum consisting entirely of a series of life-like "projects" that students would select for themselves and bring to completion in their own ways. For Kilpatrick, engagement in voluntary, purposeful activity was the only form that education should ever take. He was opposed to *any* subject matter that was "fixed in advance." Everything that a student learned was to flow naturally from volitional activity. Kilpatrick does not even mention grammar in describing his educational goals. His extreme reluctance to engage in any kind of formal instruction, however, is well illustrated by his approach to reading:

> I will have my primary children gradually live reading. To begin with, each one will, for example, have his name on his cabinet, where he keeps his various school possessions. His name he will soon learn to recognize along with the names of others near by. There will also be a bulletin board on which announcements that concern the school are daily written. Those who can, will read and live these announcements. They will also read them to the others not yet able to read, who will likewise live them.[9]

Kilpatrick was the senior professor of Educational Philosophy at Columbia between 1918 and 1938. Historian Lawrence Cremin estimates that Kilpatrick "taught some 35,000 students from every state in the Union at a time when Teachers College was training a substantial percentage of the articulate leaders of American education."[10]

Because of the influence of the more extreme doctrines, like Kilpatrick's, progressive educators quickly adopted a stance of opposition to formal instruction in grammar. From the early decades of the century to the present day, their position has not evolved. They acknowledge that students have to be trained to avoid embarrassing grammatical errors to get ahead in society, but they are opposed in principle to formal instruction in grammatical concepts. This leads them to adopt the counter-intuitive position that the less students know about grammar in theory, the more easily they can be trained to avoid "mechanical mistakes." The idea seems to be that conscious, conceptual knowledge just gets in the way of a smoothly functioning brain. Franklin Bobbitt, an influential progressive, writing in 1924 about the topic of "English Expression" argues that good vocabularies result from rich experiences, naturally, not from studying dictionaries, and then:

> A second major need is sensitive sentence-sense, and a feeling for the grammatical relationships and sequences in the make-up of the sentence. One imbibes these things from the language atmosphere in which one grows up. Except for the grammatical information needed for avoiding certain pitfalls, no great amount of systematic training is here needed.[11]

In his catalog of specific guidelines, Bobbitt's language on this point becomes more emphatic. Formal instruction in grammar is not only unnecessary, it is apparently detrimental:

> Language activities should be as unconscious and automatic as possible.
>
> One should be made conscious of only those aspects of his language of which he must be watchful for the sake of exactness and correctness.
>
> One should be left unconscious of those aspects of language which one uses properly as a result of unconscious training.[12]
>
> In the main, matters of form should be made clear only as the difficulty arises. So far as no difficulty arises in the undirected language life of the individual, he may better remain relatively unconscious of the technical language forms and relationships.[13]

Both the traditional and progressive approaches to grammar limit the subject to suit practical ends. The traditional approach, however, has more ambitious ends. It provides students with a coherent, though somewhat simplified account of the structure of all sentences. This account is designed to be helpful in mastering foreign languages and interpreting obscure sentences in one's own language, like the beginning of the Declaration of Independence. It also gives students abstract structures to use in constructing elaborate, Shakespearean sentences and a deeper explanation of "mechanical rules." Progressives limit themselves to the avoidance of stigmatized usages that sound incorrect with no account of what, if anything, lies behind their condemnation.

The progressive approach has been recycled continuously since Bobbitt's day and has always been presented as the latest pedagogy. Its current incarnation, Constance Weaver's *Teaching Grammar in Context* with its "receptive competence," has been mentioned previously.

The strange fact that the English teaching profession is opposed to formal instruction in grammar seems to me to be an example of the broader phenomenon illustrated by Professor Kilpatrick's career. Like arithmetic, grammar owes its prominence in education to the practical value of the formal mastery of its rudiments: one learns the parts of speech and the conjugation of verbs and moves on. As a prototypical, formal topic in the early years of education and the first of the liberal arts, grammar was inevitably targeted for elimination by radical progressives. Other developments were soon to add credibility to their position.

The Return of Speculative Grammar, Part 1

Charles Fries's 1952 book, *The Structure of English: An Introduction to the Construction of English Sentences*, is a basic source for educators who oppose formal instruction in grammar. As we have seen, it was cited favorably in 1991 by the NCTE handbook of research as the "strongest and most typical critique" of traditional grammar. This is an unfortunate way for *The Structure of English* to be remembered. It was a valuable contributions to the development of modern linguistics. In its harsh critique of traditional school grammar, however, it was guilty of overreaching.

In *Structure*, Fries asserts that the stylistic recommendations found in many traditional grammar books are arbitrary and often contradicted by actual usage. He takes pride in the fact that his studies are based on the practice of actual speakers and condemns "attempts to teach forms that do not occur in the actual speech of native speakers of Standard English, forms that have become shibboleths of the classroom."[14] In raising these issues, Fries was ahead of his time. As we shall see, such criticism has become a staple of books on usage in recent years but is not entirely justified. The works of the traditionalists who are the recipients of such criticism were not specifically cited by

Fries and are rarely discussed in detail by his successors. In fact, it is difficult to find an example of a prominent traditionalist laying down a genuinely arbitrary rule. Their rules are based on the usage of respected authors and speakers, a custom that is preserved by usage panels in dictionaries to the present day. They may be criticized for using too few models or being old-fashioned in their tastes, imperious in style, or simply mistaken on particular points, but there is no difference in principle between the traditional approach to correct usage and that of Fries and his successors. We will return to these points in Chapter Five.

The portion of Fries's work that did the most damage to the authority of traditional grammar is the second chapter, in which he maintains that there is no good definition of a sentence. This is an important charge since the sentence is grammar's most fundamental concept. Grammatical rules are essentially rules for writing sentences. If people really did not know what sentences were, grammar would be a radically incoherent enterprise. Yet Fries assures his readers that such is the case:

> More than two hundred different definitions of the sentence confront the worker who undertakes to deal with the structure of English utterances. The common school grammars continue to repeat the familiar definition, "A sentence is a group of words expressing a complete thought," although this ancient definition . . . quite evidently does not furnish a workable set of criteria by which to recognize sentences.[15]

Fries goes on to quote disparate definitions of sentences from textbooks and linguistic treatises—e.g., from a German scholar, John Ries: "A sentence is a grammatically constructed smallest unit of speech which expresses its content with respect to this content's relation to reality."[16] Fries's conclusion is that the nature of the sentence still awaits clarification by modern science. His approach to the problem is based on the study of the transcript of many hours of surreptitiously recorded phone calls. He hypothesizes that the points at which speakers change must mark the end of "free standing units of speech." He argues that a sentence is a single, free-standing unit of speech and sets out to ascertain their essential qualities by a comparative study of his texts. Given the limits of his data, his conclusions are all tentative.

The key to understanding Fries's statements about sentences is that he has adopted the point of view of a skeptical philosopher. Like Socrates, he is seeking an airtight definition of a sentence. Like Socrates, he can be confident that none will be forthcoming. The underlying reason is not people's inability to recognize sentences. It is that every plausible definition of a sentence contains some term like "relation to reality" that raises further problems in definition. Traditional grammar takes the understanding of such terms for granted. According to Fries, this makes it "intuitive." His desire is to replace intuitive grammar with a system that is entirely explicit and empirical.

In fact, there is a greater consensus among traditionalists on the nature of the sentence than Fries's chapter leads one to believe. The traditional definition of a sentence derives from the very beginning of Aristotle's essay, *On Interpretation*, the first essay in the *Organum:*

> Sometimes we have a thought that is not accompanied by truth or falsehood; sometimes a thought to which one or the other must belong. This is also true of speech. Truth and falsehood concern synthesis and division. Nouns and verbs by themselves are like thoughts lacking synthesis and division, e.g., "man" or "white," when nothing is added. They are neither true or false. For example, "goat-stag" [a mythological creature] signifies something, but it is not yet true or false, unless you predicate existence or non-existence of it either generally or at a particular time. . . .Every sentence has a meaning . . . but not every one is a proposition, just those that are either true or false. For example, a prayer is a sentence but is neither true or false, but let us dismiss those issues, whose examination is more closely related to rhetoric and poetry. The proposition is the subject of our current study.[17]

Though somewhat disjointed, Aristotle's remarks are wonderfully pregnant. They contain the crucial observation, elliptically expressed, of the indispensable role played in them by the union of a noun and a verb in creating a sentence. Aristotle also implies that designation of a time frame, a tense, is an essential quality of a predicate. With minor stipulations, the definition holds up perfectly well to this day and in every known language. Utterances now known as declarative sentences are, as Aristotle observed, groups of words arranged in such a way that they join a subject and a predicate and can, therefore, be judged to be true or false. Later grammarians have included questions and commands in the category of sentence. These did not concern Aristotle, since he was writing an introduction to logic, which takes only propositions into account. Nevertheless, it is not difficult to see questions and commands as variations of declarative sentences. Both include subjects and predicates and are viewed in modern terms as "transformations" of true-or-false statements. The traditional definition of the sentence as "a complete thought" seems defective only when it is detached from its context. Traditional grammars always go on to specify that "complete thoughts" consist of propositions, questions, or commands.

Aristotle's insights are still central. In the best-selling *The Language Instinct*, Steven Pinker, a leading authority on contemporary linguistics, gives a definition of the sentence that is just an updated version of Aristotle's passage. Pinker substitutes an impossible event for Aristotle's mythical goat-stag creature:

> A sentence...must express some kind of meaning that does not clearly reside in its nouns and verbs but that embraces the entire combination and turns it into a proposition that can be true or false. Take, for example, the optimistic sentence *The Red Sox will win the World Series*. The word *will* does not apply to the Red Sox alone, nor to the World Series alone, nor to winning alone; it applies to an entire concept, the-Red-Sox-winning-the-World-Series. The concept is timeless and therefore truthless. . . .But the word *will* pins the concept down to temporal coordinates. . . .If I declare "The Red Sox will win the World Series," I can be right or wrong (probably wrong, alas).[18]

The feature of the traditional definition underlying Fries's criticism is that it invokes, without explaining, our intuitive recognition of statements that could be judged true or false, questions that could be answered, or commands that could be obeyed. In stressing this shortcoming, Fries was again ahead of his time. He envisioned a grammar whose rules and definitions would be entirely explicit and empirical. The effort to formulate such a grammar is of great interest currently because it would enable computers to mimic human speech: they could be programmed to produce an infinite number of original, grammatical sentences while avoiding anomalous ones. Nor is there anything objectionable in the attempt to formulate such rules. It was, however, mistaken of Fries to assume that traditional grammar's intuitive nature compromised its pedagogical value. In much the same way, it would be an interesting challenge to try to formulate explicit definitions and rules by which a computer could be programmed to recognize tools and to separate them from pieces of junk in a garage. Research to this end, however, would not render traditional shop-class pedagogy obsolete. Unfortunately, however, Fries's critique and society's growing fixation with computer science seem to have produced a mistaken consensus among English teachers that modern linguistics has rendered the traditional definition of the sentence obsolete. I recently posed the question to the email list of the Assembly of Teachers of English Grammar—whether Aristotle's definition of a sentence was not essentially sound—and was unable to find anyone to endorse it.[19] This seems to me to be a vivid example of how the prestige of speculative grammar undermines instruction in practical grammar. Students who are told that sentences cannot be defined will inevitably find the whole subject of grammar confusing.

Fries also criticized the traditional definitions of the eight parts of speech:

> What is a "noun," for example? The usual definition is that "a noun is the name of a person, place, or thing." But blue is the "name" of a color, as is yellow or red, and yet, in the expressions a blue tie, a yellow rose, a red dress we do not call blue and yellow and red "nouns" We do call red a noun in the sentence, "This red is the shade I want."[20]

Fries was right that traditional grammarians have not been entirely consistent in their definitions of the parts of speech. The parts of speech are traditionally taught to young students, and the ways in which they have been taught reproduce the way in which classificatory schemes are usually internalized. One starts with the prototypes: the clearest, most familiar examples of a category. Children who are learning to recognize birds do not begin with an abstract definition, but with a familiar and unproblematic example of the category, like a robin. The first test of bird-hood is resemblance to robin-hood. As people grow, they refine their criteria and in the end are capable of making more or less scientific distinctions, as that an emu is, and a bat is not, a bird. But it would be a mistake pedagogically to start with emus and bats.

So, too, in teaching the classes of words, it is natural to begin with prototypical examples. Names of persons, places, and things provide a good collection of nouns. As one continues to study grammar, more refined criteria come into play, often subconsciously. Nouns are words that act like prototypical nouns. The decisive criteria of the parts of speech have to do with the rules governing their forms and the kinds of words with which they are combined. English nouns form phrases with articles (*the, a[n]*) and possessives, normally have distinctive singular and plural forms, and may be made into possessives, whereas verbs may be introduced by modal auxiliaries (*can, could, may, might, shall, should, will, would*), usually have distinctive past-tense forms, and take the suffix *-ing*. Fries deserves credit for calling attention to such features as the best basis for a taxonomy of words, though he was not the first authority to do so. In fact, William Lily and John Colet deserve credit for this innovation insofar as English is concerned. Such definitions have greater scientific validity, but people teaching grade school children about nouns are well-advised to begin with the traditional definitions.

In applying any taxonomy, one encounters borderline cases and anomalies. Fries alludes to some of the complications that arise in parts of speech. A word's part of speech is a way of referring to its function in a sentence. In English, many words can be used as more than one part of speech. Any noun, for example, can be given an adjectival function by putting it in front of another noun. We think of *chicken* as being a noun, but in a phrase like *chicken salad* it functions as an adjective. It can be distinguished from normal adjectives, however, in that it cannot itself be modified by adverbs of degree. Although we can speak of a *very good salad*, it sounds strange to say that we have a *very chicken salad*. Hence, one could have a long debate on whether the *chicken* in *chicken salad* is really a noun (acting like an adjective) or really an adjective. For all practical purposes, however, it makes no difference.

It is also true that there have been adjustments in the theory of the parts of speech over the centuries. Dionysius of Thrace classified nouns and adjectives together, because they have the same kinds of inflectional endings in Greek, and he separated participles from other forms of the verbs.

Dionysius of Thrace	*Donatus*	*Priestley*
Nouns (Adjectives)	Nouns (Adjectives)	Nouns
Verbs	Verbs	Verbs (participles)
Participles	Participles	*******
Articles	*****	Adjectives (articles)
Pronouns	Pronoun	Pronouns
Prepositions	Prepositions	Prepositions
Adverbs (Interjections)	Adverbs	Adverbs
Conjunctions	Conjunctions	Conjunctions
*****	Interjections	Interjections

Donatus dropped articles, which do not exist in Latin, and separated interjections from Dionysius' adverbs. His word classes were kept in early English grammars until Joseph Priestley in *The Rudiments of English Grammar*, in 1761, separated adjectives and nouns, while dropping participles as a separate category. Henceforth, participles were treated as forms of verbs—i.e., verbs being used as adjectives. Priestley also viewed articles as a subspecies of adjective.[21] His classification has been dominant ever since.

Fries outlined a new taxonomy. His classification was based on the places that words could occupy in sample sentences. All observed differences in possible positions resulted in new taxonomic subdivisions. For example, *not* was separated from other adverbs because of its use in the middle of compound verbs—e.g., *it may not happen*. The approach resulted in four classes of words that resembled nouns, verbs, adjectives, and adverbs, respectively, and nineteen groups of "function words." These included a number of one- or two-word categories—e.g., *yes* and *no, there, do* and *did* (when used as auxiliary verbs), *lets*, and *please*. The scheme was based on a very limited amount of data. Even so, it was obviously too complicated for practical pedagogical purposes. Had Fries continued to expand his database, the complexity of his taxonomy would have grown apace. These days, *y'-know* and *like* would have to have their own separate categories. Eventually, he would have come to resemble the grammarian in Erasmus' satire who devoted his life to understanding how the parts of speech are distinguished. In fact, he does not seem to have returned to his taxonomy. It was an interesting experiment that called attention to the distinguishing syntactic characteristics of a number of words and phrases and thereby contributed to the advance of linguistics. In contrast, it had the same kind of negative impact as his discussion of the definition of a sentence. It gave rise to the false impression that modern linguistics had rendered the traditional, eight-part taxonomy obsolete.

The Return of Speculative Grammar, Part 2

Fries was a forerunner. The modern era of speculative grammar began in earnest in 1957 with the publication of Noam Chomsky's *Syntactic Structures*. The question that Chomsky posed is unavoidable if one takes a broad view of language. All normal human beings master at least one complex language, and they are the only creatures who do so. This implies that we are born with—that our genetic compositions include—a language faculty, the distinctive, innate ability to learn a language. Chomsky's project consisted of the scientific description of this faculty. Since its nature is the very thing under investigation, it has been described in various, provisional ways. Chomsky has used the term "language acquisition device," implying, on the one hand, that the faculty can ultimately be identified with certain physical features of the brain. On the other hand, the faculty may also be viewed as a kind of knowledge. If so, the content of this innate knowledge is a "universal grammar," the rules or principles that enable us to grasp the grammar of a particular language on the basis of a relatively slight experience. Chomsky's goal has been to make the rules of this grammar explicit. As we have seen, the same goal animated the speculative grammarians of the late middle ages. As Chomsky has pointed out, his work represented a departure for linguistics in the 1950s, but it was not a radically new enterprise. Rather, it represented the re-emergence of a "long-lapsed and largely forgotten tradition."[22]

The kind of rules that Chomsky proposed are known as *generative*, or *transformational*. They represent an ordered series of choices that a speaker makes in creating a sentence. The transformational rule from which all sentences are generated is that a sentence consists of a noun phrase plus a verb phrase. Noun phrases and verb phrases may, in turn, consist of many different things. A noun phrase, for example, may consist of an article plus an adjective plus a noun. Chomsky's concepts of these elements do not differ from those of a traditional grammarian. His approach is distinct from traditional grammar in two ways. First, it is dynamic. It envisions the creation of a sentence as an orderly sequence of choices, whereas traditional grammar merely describes sentences as static structures: one word is the subject; another, the finite verb, and so forth. In Chomsky's system, some kinds of sentences are said to be derived from others. For example, questions and commands are said to be "transformations" of declarative sentences.

Second, Chomsky's grammar aims at being completely explicit, starting with the concept of a sentence and ending with a specific string of words. Traditional grammar leaves some matters out of account. It has little to say, for example, of the rules of word order in English—e.g., that indirect objects come between verbs and direct objects.

The emergence of Chomsky's grammar seemed to lend further support to the notion that traditional grammar was obsolete. Again, the impression was misleading. Like the speculative grammar of the middle ages, Chomsky's grammar is based on traditional grammar. His first rule, for example, S > NP + VP, is a symbolic rendering of Aristotle's definition of a sentence in *On Interpretation,* a sentence consists of the union of a subject and a predicate. The primacy of the declarative sentence is also found in *On Interpretation* and lies at the root of traditional grammar.

I do not mean that there was anything underhanded about Chomsky's reliance on traditional grammar. He made no secret of his use of traditional concepts. Furthermore, he explicitly stated that traditional grammar, not transformational, was an essential component of a good education. He made this remark in connection with a brief essay, "A Defense of Grammar," by Frederica Davis, who wrote, in part:

> I believe that traditional grammar, the eight parts of speech, mechanics, and usage, should comprise about one fifth of every middle school child's study of the English language. . . . Traditional grammar should be taught in a systematic, sequential way, using the child's own written work whenever possible.[23]

Realizing that traditional grammar was thought obsolete because of Chomsky's work, Davis sent him a copy of her essay for comment.

Replying at some length, Chomsky affirmed the educational importance of traditional grammar:

> I hesitate to express a judgment on the main question you are addressing, simply from lack of relevant knowledge. My uninformed guess would be that the study of grammar would have little detectable effect on writing ability, but I think that it should be taught for its own intrinsic interest and importance. I don't see how any person can truly be called "educated" who doesn't know the elements of sentence structure, or who doesn't understand the nature of a relative clause, a passive construction, and so on. Furthermore, if one is going to discuss literature, including here what students write themselves, and to come to understand how it is written and why, these conceptual tools are indispensable.
>
> For these purposes, I think traditional grammar so-called (say, the grammar of Jespersen) remains today a very impressive and useful basis for such teaching. I can't see any reason for teaching structural grammars of English, or for teaching transformational grammar in the manner of some instructional books that I have seen.[24]

Despite this advice, a number of writers have attempted to devise revolutionary approaches to elementary grammar inspired by structural linguistics and transformational grammar. The result is that even teachers who agree that grammar should be taught disagree on methodology and terminology. As in the days of King Henry VIII, there are as many doctrines as there are teachers, and this leads to the "great encumbrance and confusion of young and tender wits."

The Empirical Evidence Against Formal Instruction in Grammar

Starting in the early sixties, opponents of formal instruction in grammar have adopted an aggressive stance, stating that empirical research has proven that such instruction, far from helping student writing, is actually harmful to it. This assertion is based on three studies, summaries of earlier research, the Braddock report of 1963, the Hillocks report of 1986, and the Hillocks and Smith report of 1991. The authors of these studies and those who cite them express dismay that their conclusions are resisted by many teachers who go on teaching traditional grammar despite "scientific proof" that they are wasting time and effort. This is not really so surprising since the Braddock–Hillocks position is counter-intuitive. In virtually all endeavors, it helps to have a clear conceptual understanding of relevant data and relationships. Why should language be so different?

A glance at the studies summarized by Braddock and by Hillocks clears up the mystery: All of them concern the short-term effects of instruction in formal grammar on the work of relatively mature students. For this reason, these studies have no real bearing on the value of the traditional approach to teaching grammar. From antiquity to the twentieth century, grammar was introduced to children at the beginning of their schooling, as soon as they learned how to read, and it remained a central concern for several years. It was a foundation that was built carefully and gradually in the still-receptive minds of relatively young pupils. The question to be asked then is whether a foundation of grammatical concepts laid slowly and systematically in the early grades is beneficial to students later in their academic careers. Instead of addressing that question, the research projects cited by Braddock and by Hillocks ask what happens when you insert some grammar into the curriculum at various spots along the way. This is like trying to insert partial foundations beneath half-finished houses and concluding from the ensuing debacles that foundations are useless.

Moreover, grammar is a difficult subject—elementary but difficult, like arithmetic. The inclusion of a difficult subject in a curriculum at any point is bound to have an adverse short-term effect on student performances in related subjects simply because students have a finite amounts of time and energy. If we make students jog for a mile every morning, we will find that they have less energy on the playground at lunch, but this does not mean that jogging is bad for their long-term physical conditioning.

Hillocks and Smith concede that most of the studies they cite are susceptible to the criticism that the training periods involved were "comparatively short" and the "amount of grammar instruction small."[25] In their view, however, the great exception to this generalization, "by far the most impressive" study in the case against formal grammar is one completed by one W. B. Elley of the New Zealand Council for Educational Research and his colleagues from Aorere College. The study was published originally in the *New Zealand Journal of Educational Studies* in 1975. Because of the importance attached to the results, it was then reprinted in *Research in the Teaching of English*, an NCTE publication. The progress of 248 high school students in eight different classes was monitored by yearly essay tests and comprehensive English tests for three years. Three of the classes studied transformational grammar, three focused in reading and writing assignments with no formal grammar, and two sections used a textbook that contained traditional grammar. No significant difference turned up in the testing among the three groups.

The Elley study exhibits the shortcomings mentioned above. No account is given of the students' earlier training in grammar. The possibility is not excluded that the traditional grammar class merely repeated material that the students had already learned in grade school. If so, it could not be expected to lead to a dramatic improvement in their writing. Even apart from such considerations, the Elley experiment had little relevance to the pedagogical value of traditional grammar. In the experiment, the transformational grammar group used the experimental Oregon curriculum, which was implemented conscientiously. Care was taken to see that the students grasped the ideas underlying transformational grammar. In contrast, the books employing traditional grammar consisted of an unheralded series, "Let's Learn English" by P. R. Smart. No special effort was made to see that the concepts of traditional grammar were well taught: "Exercises were chosen from [the P. R. Smart] texts whenever they were deemed suitable by the teachers."[26] Indeed, Elley and his co-authors acknowledge that the evaluation of traditional grammar was not a primary goal. "The main purpose of this investigation," they write, "was to determine the direct effects of a study of transformational grammar on the language growth of secondary school pupils."[27] This important fact is not mentioned by Hillocks and Smith, who make the Elley study the mainstay of his case against traditional grammar.

One study, that by William H. Macauley, "The difficulty of grammar," published in England in 1947, does question the value of teaching grammar consistently from the early grades on. Macauley is not cited in the Braddock report or the Hillocks report, but his work is mentioned in the Hillocks–Smith essay on grammar and usage in the 1991 *Handbook of Research on Teaching the English Language Arts,* and it has since then become an important exhibit in the case against grammar. On Macauley's account, the study of formal grammar was a mainstay of Scottish elementary schools. Starting at age seven-and-a-half, pupils studied the parts of speech and sentence structure in systematic progression for about a half an hour a day. Nevertheless, he says, language teachers in high school "are finding that the pupils entering the secondary school appear to show a complete lack of understanding of even the terms of grammar."[28]

Macauley gave tests on the identification of parts of speech to 131 twelve-year-olds. The test consisted of fifty sentences with one word underlined. Pupils were asked to pick the part of speech of the underlined word. Their choices were: noun, pronoun, adjective, verb, and adverb. Macauley reports mean scores for the five different parts of speech and for the test as a whole. The last figure was 27.9% correct. In other words, the average student missed nearly three-fourths of the questions. Macauley gave versions of the same test to high school students. The scores improved somewhat, but clearly typical students were still confused about parts of speech despite their training. Macauley's conclusion is that formal grammar should not be taught in grade school, "as it appears to be time wasted," or in junior high school, "as comparatively few pupils have the necessary maturity and intelligence [to benefit from it]." In senior high school, he says, "formal grammar might be reserved for the best classes, which are usually those following a purely academic course."[29]

Taken at face value, Macauley's study suggests that the parts of speech are impossible for normal people to understand. If he is correct, this means that two thousand years of western education have been a charade. The elementary textbooks of Dionysius Thrax, Donatus, Priscian, and Lily—to say nothing of the grammatical notes in modern dictionaries—have never been understood by any outside of a small, intellectual elite.

If Macauley's experiment is valid, one should be able to replicate his results with any group of students, including those in schools where the study of grammar is said to flourish. The study is easy to replicate. All one needs to do is administer a short, multiple-choice test. A school where grammar flourishes is Elm Grove Lutheran in the suburbs of Milwaukee. In this school, "formal grammar" is taught to seventh- and eighth-graders by a dedicated teacher named Paul Greutzmacher. I have spoken with several of his former students who testify to the positive impact of his instruction in grammar on their intellectual and professional development. Greutzmacher is an idealistic man who decided that his calling was to be a teacher, but he nearly gave up on this career because he did not understand grammar. Having gotten some guidance from a senior colleague and an appropriate book, he mastered the subject himself and has been joyfully sharing his knowledge with grade school students ever since.

Greutzmacher gave the Macauley test to thirty-seven of his students. Their mean score was 78 percent. One of Greutzmacher's pupils had a perfect score; another thirteen had scores of 86 percent or better. None of Macauley's 131 students scored this well.

One would like to know what lay behind Macauley's results. Part of the explanation is that the words that he chose for classification were deliberately confusing. In one version of his test, for example, *last* is underlined in three different sentences—used as a noun, a verb, and an adjective, respectively. To make matters worse, Macauley's test does not state whether questions pertain to the normal use of underlined words or to their use in the given sentences. Greutzmacher and I retained the syntax of Macauley's sentences but avoided individual words with multiple functions, like *last*. Still, even considering the special difficulty of the test, the Scottish performance was remarkably poor. It may mean that the teachers involved used very ineffective methods in teaching grammar, or perhaps the students who took the test were just not trying. Macauley does not say whether they had any incentive to do well.

The NCTE History of Grammar

The Hillocks–Smith essay in the 1991 *Handbook of Research* embellishes its case against grammar with a jaundiced view of the history of grammar in education. Here we encounter the startling assertion that grammar was invented by Greeks in the Hellenistic period because they could no longer read their own archaic literature. The Hellenistic grammarians, we are told, found themselves with a collection of books "filled with language they could no longer understand."[30] It is not reassuring to find an error like this in a reputable academic publication. A steady stream of allusions to Homer and other early authors in Hellenistic literature makes it unmistakably clear to anyone with even a passing acquaintance with the primary texts that the earliest classics were read, understood, and appreciated by literate Greeks continuously throughout antiquity. Like the other sciences that the Greeks developed, grammar was not invented to enable them to *do* something, but to do something *better*, with conscious control. As bronze armor made them better warriors, so grammar enabled them to understand ancient poetry better, appreciate its artistry, catalog the peculiarities of ancient dialects, analyze meters, correct scribal errors in manuscripts, recognize interpolations, assign authorship to anonymous fragments, and so forth—in short, to practice philology.

Hillocks and Smith never mention philology in their survey of the uses of grammar by the Greeks. Nor do they explain exactly how grammar, which they treat as a pseudo-science, enabled the Greeks to decode those supposedly unintelligible texts. However it did so, they apparently think it quickly outlived its usefulness. On the Hillocks–Smith view, grammar continued to enjoy great, though undeserved, prestige during the middle ages because of a murky association between it and revealed religion, but it is better to let Hillocks and Smith speak for themselves:

> The beginning point of education in the seven liberal arts was the word. Grammar became, for most of the Middle Ages, the chief subject of the trivium (grammar, rhetoric, and logic), which was the key to the quadrivium. Grammar was the "gateway" to all knowledge, particularly sacred knowledge. "Grammar was thought to discipline the mind and the soul at the same time, honing the intellectual and

spiritual abilities that the future cleric would need to read and speak with discernment" (Huntsman, 1983, p. 59). The major task of the cleric according to Morrison (1983), was to use the arts, chief of which was grammar, first "to disclose the hidden mysteries of Scripture; and, second, to express esoteric doctrine for the wise while disguising it from the simple without falsifying it" (p. 38). . . The object of education then involved the near paradox of revealing the hidden truth of Scripture by means of arts that are themselves cloaked in error. In the Middle Ages grammar was the key to the entire enterprise.

"The near paradox"?

The grain of truth in this account is that in the middle ages speakers of vernacular tongues had to learn Latin grammar in order to read books, because they were all written in Latin. The books that grammar made accessible included the Latin version of the Bible. It is, however, a gross distortion to imply that medieval scholars attributed mystic powers to grammar. Then, as now, grammar provided the tools by which one could consciously analyze the meaning of sentences and master a non-native language. What animates the grammarian is a desire for conscious understanding. It is the antithesis of the quest for mystic edification depicted by Hillocks and Smith.

The Scandal of Prescriptivism

The study of grammar helps us to understand the great literature of the past and to speak and write eloquently. The second function, grammar as a "prescriptive" discipline, is hard to represent sympathetically at the present time. The rules of language are essentially arbitrary and constantly changing. Usages that are considered incorrect today will be perfectly proper tomorrow. For the present, "mistakes" occur most frequently in the speech of the young and the dialects of the poor and of racial and ethnic minorities. These facts have contributed to a negative stereotype. Concern with correct speech is taken as a sign that a person is a despotic, reactionary old fogey, indifferent to social justice and contemptuous of cultural diversity. The stereotype is unfair: there is a strong case that the dissemination of "good" grammar confers substantial benefits, individual and collective. Nevertheless, the stereotype is well-established and everyone who writes about grammar has to fear being labeled a "prescriptivist" even though human languages are nothing but arrays of arbitrary rules, fabrics of prescriptions. Several issues have been clouded as a result.

From the point of humanity as a whole, the most important benefit of the prevalence of good grammar is that it contributes to the preservation and spread of standard languages. They are a blessing that we all take for granted, but probably should not. I subscribe via the Internet to a scholarly journal in Classics, *Electronic Antiquity,* whose main offices are in the University of Tasmania. The essays it contains are as readily intelligible to me as newsletters printed on my own campus in Wisconsin. The effortless global reach enjoyed by speakers of standard English in every walk of life, which this fact illustrates, did not just happen. As E. D. Hirsch, Jr. points out in *Cultural Literacy,* medieval Europe was a patchwork of mutually unintelligible and rapidly evolving dialects. "If you traveled four villages away instead of three you might not be able to understand what people were saying."[31] A famous anecdote transmitted by William Caxton (1422?–91), a translator and the father of English book-printing, illustrates this assertion. In the preface to his *Eneydos* (a translation of a French paraphrase of the *Aeneid*), Caxton writes:

> My Lord Abbot of Westminster did do show to me lately certain evidences written in old English, for to reduce it into our English now used. And certainly it was written in such wise that it was more like to Dutch than English, I could not reduce ne bring it to be understood. And certainly our language now used varieth far from that which was used and spoken when I was born. For we Englishmen be born under the domination of the moon, which is never steadfast but ever wavering, waxing one season and waneth and decreaseth another season. And that common English that is spoken in one shire varieth from another, insomuch that in my days happened that certain merchants were in a ship in Thames for to have sailed over the sea into Zealand, and for lack of wind they tarried at Foreland, and went to land for to refresh them. And one of them named Sheffield, a mercer, came into a house and asked for meat, and especially he asked after eggs; and the good wife answered that she could speak no French, and the merchant was angry, for he also could speak no French, but would have had eggs, and she understood him not. And then at last another said, that he would have "eyren"; then the goodwife said that she understood him well. Lo, what should a man in these days now write, eggs or eyren? Certainly it is hard to please every man because of the diversity and change of language.[32]

Around Caxton's time, the obvious economic, social, and cultural advantages of uniting large numbers of people together by a common tongue inspired a series of enlightened and largely successful efforts to create standard national languages. In southern Europe, this was accomplished through government-sponsored academies, the Accademia della Crusca founded in 1582 to perfect the Tuscan dialect, Cardinal Richelieu's French academy in 1630, and the Spanish Academy in 1713.

The creation of a standard language posed a particularly difficult problem among the free-spirited English and their cousins in the United States. Who had the right to tell these people how to speak and write? Proposals to establish linguistic academies died aborning in both countries. But capitalism provided a different, equally effective solution. In both countries, best-selling dictionaries and grammars achieved a degree of authority that probably could not have been conferred by political authorities. The first authoritative English dictionary was Samuel Johnson's, which was published in 1755. Noah Webster performed the same service for American English in 1806. And the same period saw the rise of books on proper English grammar. In England, the most influential was one by Bishop Robert Lowth, *A Short Introduction to English Grammar*, which went through twenty-two editions between its initial publication in 1762 and 1800. In addition, a million copies of Lindley Murray's adaptation of Lowth's work, *English Grammar*, were sold in America. Thus, it was in the eighteenth and early-nineteenth centuries that "good English" became a widespread preoccupation, that the first little child was scolded for saying, "Me and him went to the store."

The importance of the grammatical aspect of creating standard English should not be underestimated. People who work with foreign languages are well aware that obstacles to comprehension are generated as least as often by grammatical difficulties as by the meanings of individual words. Caxton's passage cited above illustrates the point. Although the spelling of individual words has been modernized for the reader's convenience, it was not really necessary to do so. Modern readers could have easily guessed the meaning of "mete and eggys," for example. The most obscure point in the passage is whether "for to have sayled to zeland" means that the merchants were returning from Zeeland or were setting out for it. That is a grammatical obscurity.

In any event, by dint of honest efforts, Samuel Johnson, Bishop Lowth, and individuals like them contributed significantly to the creation of modern standard English, with all of its benefits. One might think, therefore, that these pioneers would be respected, if not revered, for what they did. In fact, the lexicographers are spoken of with respect, but modern linguists and pedagogues have made grammarians like Lowth the butts of ridicule. An example is Steven Pinker's chapter on "The Language Mavens," in *The Language Instinct*. Pinker is generally unimpressed by the phenomenon of standardized languages. He explicitly endorses a remark attributed to linguist Max Weinrich that a standard language is a dialect with an army and a navy.[33] In fact, there are important differences between standard languages and dialects. A standard language has a written literature with classical works, dictionaries and grammars, and systems of education. From 31 B.C. to A.D. 376, Greek was the standard language of the eastern Mediterranean even though the armies and navies were controlled by Latin speakers in Rome. And Latin remained the standard language of Europe long after the barbarians had taken over militarily. Tuscan became Italy's standard dialect in the absence of political unity—i.e., without an army and a navy.

In Pinker's terms, a language maven is an excessively judgmental critic of the language of others. One who speaks disparagingly of double negatives, for example, would qualify. John Simon and William Safire are flagrant mavens. According to Pinker, the phenomenon of the language maven began in the eighteenth century. In saying this, he is referring to the popularity of books like Lowth's, but he does not cite specific authors or passages. His tactic is to disparage the whole effort to standardize English grammar by selecting a couple of anonymous examples that serve his purpose.

> Latin was still considered the language of enlightenment and learning . . . and it was offered as an ideal of precision and logic to which English should aspire. . . .Most of the hobgoblins of contemporary prescriptive grammar (don't split infinitives, don't end a sentence with a preposition) can be traced back to these eighteenth century fads. Of course, forcing modern speakers of English to not—whoops, not to splint an infinitive because it is not done in Latin makes about as much sense as forcing modern residents of England to wear laurels and togas.[34]

Pinker's polemic is a lively rendition of attitudes and arguments that have been commonplace in language arts pedagogy for many years. A case in point is provided by Julius N. Hook, the author of an otherwise very useful *History of the English Language* and a professor at the University of Illinois. We learn from the inside cover of his book that he served as the executive secretary of the NCTE, the coordinator of Project English for the U.S. Office of Education, and the director of a number of federal projects aimed at improving the preparation of teachers of secondary school English. He was also the author or co-author of three other books on teaching English. Hook's attitude toward Lowth is not difficult to divine. For example, he refers to "pronunciamentos, largely arbitrary, [which] have echoed through hundreds of thousands of classrooms since Bishop Lowth's time." Like Pinker, Hook refrains from citing specific passages in Lowth's grammar.

> If these prescriptions and proscriptions had been accurate in describing the ways that educated people actually used the language, they would be less subject to criticism. But most of them were actually only statements about how the self-anointed grammarians believed the language should be used.[35]

Lowth's work is readily available in a reprint produced by Scolar Press Limited. A hundred and eighty-six pages in length, it contains definitions of grammar, the parts of speech, the syntax of sentences, and rules for pronunciation. By far the largest portion of the work is devoted to a description of English grammar, not to a catalog of solecisms. With some updating, it could be used today to give college students a needed overview of English grammar. For example, few contemporary students know what it means to "conjugate a verb," much less how to do it. For this reason, I have often experimented with different ways of summarizing the tenses of the English verb. Lowth's presentation of this potentially confusing topic is one of the best that I have seen. The tenses of the English verb, he says, refer to the present, past, or future (I) indeterminately (I love, I loved, I shall or will love) or (II) with some particular distinction, either (A) passing (I am loving, I was loving, I shall or will be loving) or (B) finished (I have loved, I had loved, I shall or will have loved).

When he turns to questions of usage, Lowth's approach is a far cry from the caricature found in Pinker and in Hook. For example, the first point taken up is the definite article. He says that a noun without any article is taken in its widest sense. "Thus man means all mankind; as, 'The proper study of mankind is man.'" Then, in a footnote, he criticizes the King James translation of a sentence in *Acts xxii.4*. There St. Paul acknowledges that he formerly persecuted Christians "unto the death." Lowth comments, "The Apostle does not mean any particular sort of death, but death in general: the definite article therefore is improperly used. It ought to be unto death, without any article: agreeably with the original, *achri thanatou.*"[36] Thus, Lowth's actual procedure does not differ in principle from what everybody does, viz., we all infer rules of proper word usage from our reading and conversation and then judge some utterances to be defective by the standards that we have found implicit in the language.

Lowth's examples are taken from exalted writings, the King James Bible or the works of authors like Milton, Pope, Swift, and Dryden. This is a difference from contemporary linguists like Pinker, who cites the prologue to Star Trek to prove that split infinitives can be elegant and the *Ghostbusters* song as evidence that *whom* is obsolescent. But that is a matter of taste. The notion that Lowth and his contemporaries subscribed to some general doctrine that modern linguistics has overturned is simply untrue.

Lowth does talk about ending sentences with prepositions, but readers expecting him to wax vitriolic on this point will be disappointed:

> This is an idiom which our language is strongly inclined to [*note, he does not write: "to which our language is strongly inclined"*]; it prevails in common conversation and suits very well with the familiar style in writing; but the placing of the preposition before the relative is more graceful, as well as more perspicuous; and agrees much better with the solemn and elevated style.[37]

There is no warrant for the belief that Lowth wanted to stretch English to fit the rules of Latin grammar. The specific question of applying Latin rules to English arises in connection with absolute phrases—e.g., *"The door being shut,* Jesus stood in their midst." Lowth insists that pronouns in such phrases must be in the nominative case, not the objective, and takes the classicist Bentley to task for changing an absolute phrase in Milton, "he defending" to "him defending" by analogy with Latin. "This comes," Lowth says, "of forcing the English under the rules of a foreign language, *with which it has little concern* [emphasis added]."[38]

Nothing epitomizes the faults of traditional grammar in its critics' eyes better than a supposed rule against splitting infinitives, which is always cited as an instance of traditional grammar's irrational conviction that English should obey the rules of Latin. The traditional grammarians who are said to have defended this principle are never mentioned by name. Although the prohibition against splitting infinitives is used by Pinker to typify the prescriptivism of the eighteenth century, the first reference to the rule that I have been able to find occurs in the work of Henry Alford, dean of Canterbury, in 1864, well into the nineteenth century. In a book entitled *A Plea for the Queen's English,* Alford mentions in passing that a correspondent has defended the insertion of an adverb between the sign of the infinitive mood and the verb and continues:

> He gives as an instance, "to scientifically illustrate." But surely this is
> a practice entirely unknown to English speakers and writers. It seems
> to me that we ever regard the to of the infinitive as inseparable from
> its verb.[39]

It should be noted that Alford's argument is based on the usage of English speakers. He does not say that infinitives should not be split in English because they are represented by one word in Latin. It is true that Alford's impression of English usage was not entirely accurate. Split infinitives occurred, though rarely, in English literature before the end of the eighteenth century and have become progressively more common since then.[40] Careful writers resist splitting infinitives, though their resistance has nothing to do with an attempt to imitate Latin. *To*'s only function in an infinitive phrase is to indicate the syntax of the verb; as Alford says, it is the sign of the infinitive mood. Therefore, it is usually placed next to the verb and sounds strange if it separated from it for no reason. Occasions do arise, however, when it is advantageous to interpose an adverb, and careful authors have always done so.[41]

To be fair, Pinker does identify a number of mistaken criticisms of common usage by writers in the popular press. For example, his defense of the use of *hopefully* as a sentence adverb like *frankly* is perfectly reasonable. But it should be said that the prevalence of such pseudo-experts is a symptom of the fact that the general public lacks a firm understanding of grammar. The notion that there is something wrong with *hopefully* would not have gained such currency among people with a better grasp of English syntax. Such people are aware that introductory adverbs are routinely used to characterize the tone of whole sentences. In other instances, as in his defense of *between you and I,* Pinker seems less persuasive,[42] but these are matters on which reasonable people can disagree.

My problem with Pinker's influential presentation is one of emphasis, not principle. He resolves every issue in favor of spontaneous usage, thus giving the impression that all conscious efforts to speak or write "correctly" are vain and pretentious. Students who let themselves be guided by him are likely to infer that they can become excellent writers without the aid of dictionaries and grammars with all their silly rules. In fact, writing well involves the conscious mastery of countless prescriptions, as Pinker's own text constantly demonstrates. Consider just the opening two sentences of *The Language Instinct:*

> As you are reading these words, you are taking part in one of the wonders of the natural world. For you and I belong to a species with a remarkable ability: we can shape events in each other's brains with exquisite precision.

These sentences betray an understanding of the proper use of the present progressive tense, the demonstrative *this/these* and colons, of the relative independence of clauses introduced by *for,* as opposed to *because,* of the possessive case of *each other.* Pinker goes on to say that it is our "language instinct" that allows us to "shape events in each other's brains with exquisite precision." That we can communicate with our instinctive abilities is undeniable; that we can do so "with exquisite precision" on the basis of instinct alone is doubtful.

The fashionable bashing of presciptivism has made language arts teachers apologetic about teaching "correct" English to their students, especially those who speak dialects or foreign languages at home. It is good for English teachers to be trained to avoid hurting children's feelings by saying or implying that they are stupid because of the way that they have learned to speak at home. In general, nowadays, the scrupulously tactful efforts to teach standard English are justified on the grounds that it is the dialect spoken by people with money and influence.[43] The argument is that students who want good jobs need to curry favor with employers and supervisors by adopting the dialect of the elite rather than the one that they might otherwise speak. In a way, the point is well-taken. A well-turned phrase *is* often an effective way to win favorable notice. On the other hand, it has always seemed to me to be an unnecessarily cynical approach, implying that knowledge of standard English is a superficial attainment, useful but not intrinsically valuable. It is like telling students to cultivate their sex appeal if they want to get ahead.

In fact, there are better, or at least nobler, reasons to learn and respect standard English. Its existence not only promotes economic prosperity; it has social and cultural benefits as well. The spread of standard English through schools has retarded the rate of change in the English language. As Hirsch points out, linguist Henry Sweet, the model for Shaw's Professor Henry Higgins, predicted in the nineteenth century that the English, the Australians, and the Americans would be speaking mutually incomprehensible languages by 1980.[44] Thanks in part to the efforts of people like Samuel Johnson and Robert Lowth, this has not happened. In mastering and using standard English, we participate in a collective effort that has given us effortless access to the thoughts of hundreds of millions of people separated by great distances of space and time. The last person to belittle its importance of this development should be a best-selling author. Without standard English, language change would have long since left Shakespeare's works, for example, unintelligible to most English speakers and certainly to Americans and Tasmanians.

As the Max Weinrich quotation shows, contemporary linguists like to say that spoken dialects can express their speakers' thoughts as well as a standard language. This is a half truth. Spoken dialects are governed by grammatical rules that are just as elegant as those of a standard language and just as capable of producing an unlimited number of statements. There is no reason to doubt that oral dialects express the same range of logical relationships as standard languages, even though long, complex sentences are rare in them because they lack written models and books on grammar to inspire complexity. Also, spoken dialects have relatively tiny vocabularies. Deficient vocabularies may not prevent speakers from expressing everyday feelings, but fully developed ones enable them to express themselves with much greater precision and on a wider range of subjects. When Cicero wrote his speeches and essays in Latin, he had to borrow the terms for history, philosophy, poetry, comedy, tragedy, rhetoric, architecture, music, and grammar, and their technical vocabularies, from the Greek language, and we have borrowed them from his Latin. Such large-scale importation of words with complicated meanings requires the assistance of a written language. It is true that speakers of oral dialects could in principle discuss history, philosophy, and the rest in their own dialects, but to do so they would first have to learn a standard language well enough to borrow its terminology. In short, the common-sense intuition is perfectly correct. Though dialects have the same theoretical capacities as standard languages, learning one of the latter greatly increases the number and complexity of the thoughts that one can actually express.

Attitudes toward traditional grammar and spoken dialects have been endowed with political significance. Champions of standard language are supposedly motivated by the desire to preserve class structure. In their ideal world, it is implied, people who were not born into the right kind of family would not speak the right dialect and would be automatically debarred from advancement in society. In this regard, too, the truth is more complicated. The practical advantages of a standard language are overwhelming. An advanced, industrial society in which politics, education, and commerce would be conducted in a patchwork of different dialects is scarcely imaginable. Given the inevitability of a standard language, a school system that teaches it is a progressive institution. Schoolmarms may be faulted for spreading an exaggerated notion of the inferiority of dialectical speech, but their efforts make it possible for people born on the wrong side of the tracks to rise to the highest levels of wealth and influence. This is the ostensible purpose of universal schooling, and it is never served more directly than in the teaching of a standard language. Traditional British grammar schools, often characterized in this connection as protectors of privilege, actually have an enviable record of providing education for impoverished students. This is documented by Foster Watson in *The Old Grammar Schools*. Watson quotes the 1540 declaration of Archbishop Cranmer on the policy of admissions to the grammar school attached to the Cathedral of Canterbury. Some of the directors of the school wished to limit admissions to "gentlemen's" children. Cranmer asserted that poor men's children often have superior natural gifts and are more likely to be industrious students. Hence, the archbishop decreed, "If the gentleman's son be apt to learning, let him be admitted; if not apt, let the poor man's child, that is apt, enter his room."[45] Throughout their history, English grammar schools provided scholarships for the poor. Watson mentions a number of distinguished Englishmen who rose from inauspicious beginnings to great heights thanks to the grammar schools.[46] Of these, Edmund Spenser is best known to American readers.

When I questioned her on this topic, a friend of mine who teaches English as a Second Language (ESL) and linguistics told me that she carefully refrained from criticizing nonstandard English in the classroom and felt that it was important to do so. Then she added as a humorous aside, a throw-away line, that "of course" she policed her own daughters' grammar with fanatical vigilance. It was, I thought, a moment of truth. People who use "good grammar" do not hesitate to force it on the children they love. In view of this, I often find myself annoyed by contemporary linguists who have made traditional English teachers objects of ridicule. Pinker, for example, refers to dangling participles, split infinitives, and the "other hobgoblins of the schoolmarm."[47] He is a brilliant linguist and author, but for teaching my children English, I'll take the schoolmarm.

The Myth of the Bad Old Days

As previously mentioned, there is a group within the NCTE, the Assembly for the Teaching of English Grammar, or ATEG, that advocates greater emphasis on grammar in the language arts. The group is small but gradually growing in numbers and influence. As more and more state standards prescribe the teaching of grammar, its stock is destined to rise. In my opinion, however, the ATEG's efficacy at the present time is limited by its own members' negative view of traditional instruction in grammar. As a general rule, they take it for granted that the traditional teaching of grammar was radically flawed and that what is needed is not just a restoration of grammar but the discovery of some new way to teach it. There is little agreement on what this new approach should be. As in Erasmus' time, there are as many grammars as grammarians.

The assumption that traditional instruction in grammar was essentially misguided seems to me to be the mirror image of the myth of the good old days. It is not true that English classes before the sixties were generally ineffective. Many people alive today attribute their success in large part to training received in such classes. There is little to be said in defense of dull, repetitive drills or teachers who inspire only fear and loathing in their students, but these are not the exclusive properties of traditional English classes. There is no proof that the principles that guided traditional grammar must be replaced on a wholesale basis. Today's teachers can make improvements in detail, and they can take advantage of technology. For basic approaches, however, I would urge them to consider the strengths of textbooks of the past before resorting to innovations.

No texts better embody traditional school grammar than those by Alonzo Reed and Brainerd Kellogg, teachers of English grammar at the Brooklyn Collegiate and Polytechnic Institute. The more elementary of their two books, *Graded Lessons in English*, went through twenty-five editions between 1875 and 1911; the other, *Higher Lessons in English*, appeared twenty-one times between 1878 and 1913.[48]

Reed and Kellogg were reacting to the criticism that available grammar books consisted of nothing but long lists of rules to memorize. They used an inductive approach, presenting concepts with a minimum of explanation, giving students many sample sentences to analyze, and directing them to make up their own illustrative sentences.

The sample sentences in Reed and Kellogg's works have an elegance that modern texts would do well to emulate. For example, Lesson 81 in *Higher Lessons* consists entirely of aphorisms that the student is asked to analyze grammatically, by diagramming if the teacher prefers. These include:

Of all sad words of tongue or pen the saddest are these: "It might have been."

—Whittier

I fear three newspapers more than a hundred-thousand bayonets.

—Napoleon

He that allows himself to be a worm must not complain if he is trodden on.

—Kant

It is better to write one word upon the rock than a thousand on the water or the sand.

—Gladstone

In recent years, educational researchers who are skeptical of traditional school grammar have reported that some improvement in student writing can be obtained through a new kind of exercise called "sentence combining." Students are given kernel sentences and asked to combine them into longer units. An advocate of sentence combining provides this example from his class for college freshmen:

Kernel sentences:

Generals took control of Turkey.

Generals took control in a coup.

The coup was swift.

The coup was bloodless.

The coup sent personnel carriers sweeping through the cities.

The coup sent tanks sweeping through the cities.

The coup sent jeeps sweeping through the cities.

The cities were major.

The personnel carriers were armored.

A typical student response:

Tanks, personnel carriers, and jeeps were sent sweeping through a number of major cities, as Generals took control of Turkey in a swift bloodless coup.[49]

The Reed and Kellogg text provides students with many opportunities for very similar work. There is a difference, however. The use of grammatical concepts allows the student much more room for creativity. In Lesson 66, for example, after cataloging kinds of adverbial clauses, Reed and Kellogg ask students to complete sentences on their own with adverbial clauses of given types. For example:

The leaves of the water-maple turn red—*time.*

The Bunker Hill Monument stands—*place.*

The lion springs upon its prey—*manner.*

Though this exercise is within the capacity of relatively young students who understand grammatical concepts, it is an interesting challenge even for a mature writer. "The leaves of the water-maple turned red"—*as the days grew short?—while Father's hair turned gray?* By way of contrast, if one's whole purpose were to invent a dull exercise, it would be hard to beat those Turkish generals.

Throughout their books, Reed and Kellogg use the system of sentence diagramming that has become associated with their names. In fact, their approach represents a refinement of a method that appeared in an 1849 book by Stephan Clark, *Practical Grammar Illustrated by a Complete System of Diagrams.*[50] The major difference is that Clark's diagrams consist of balloons, whereas Reed and Kellogg use lines. Though Reed and Kellogg's diagrams enjoyed widespread classroom use subsequently, few published textbooks featured them until the appearance of Kolln's *Understanding English Grammar* in 1982 and Mark Lester's *Grammar and Usage in the Classroom* in 1990.

At the heart of every Reed and Kellogg diagram is a horizontal line bisected by a perpendicular. This represents the union of the sentence's indispensable elements: a subject and a finite verb. It is a visual representation of Aristotle's observation that every sentence is a synthesis of two elements: a noun (or a pronoun) and a verb. Adjectives, adverbs, and prepositional phrases are placed on diagonal lines beneath the words that they modify. A perpendicular line that stops at the horizontal divides verbs from direct objects. Object and subject complements are indicated by tilted lines. With a few additional embellishments, these basic rules make it possible to represent the grammatical relationships of a vast majority of words in normal discourse. Virtually every clause in every complete sentence has as its nucleus one of four basic structures that Reed and Kellogg's diagrams distinguish:

1. A transitive verb with a direct object—e.g., *Little strokes fell great oaks.* (Benjamin Franklin)

Figure 4–1

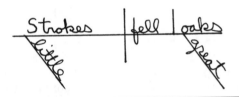

2. An intransitive or passive verb—e.g., *Women and elephants never forget.* (Dorothy Parker)

Figure 4–2

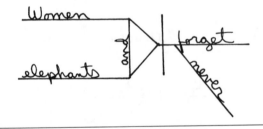

3. A linking verb with a subject complement or "predicate nominative"—e.g., *Comparisons are odious.* (Christopher Marlowe)

Figure 4–3

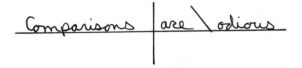

4. A factitive verb, one linking a direct object and an object complement—e.g., *The truth shall set you free.* (St. John's Gospel).[51]

Figure 4–4

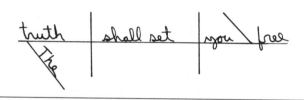

Of course, many usages occur that require further explanation. For example, sentences in mature prose often contain dependent clauses. In Reed and Kellogg's diagrams, these are connected to the main clause of the sentence by a broken line that reflects the syntactical relationship between clauses. Often the word in the main clause to which the relative pronoun refers runs between a relative pronoun and its "antecedent." In my own teaching, I depart from the practice of Reed and Kellogg—and partially revive Clark's—by enclosing dependent clauses in balloons to distinguish them more clearly from main clauses:

He jests at scars that never felt a wound.

—(William Shakespeare)

Figure 4–5

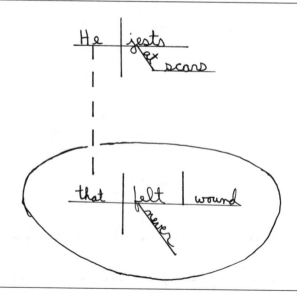

Participles, gerunds, and infinitives introduce further complications because they have dual functions, combining the work of verbs with that of adjectives, nouns, and—in the case of infinitive—even adverbs. The conventions used in dealing with them, however, are merely common-sense extensions of the basic ideas described above and are easily mastered, when properly taught, by grade school students, who can find the details of such rules fascinating. Gerunds, for example, are placed on platforms. In this way, the object of a gerund is visually distinct from elements governed by the finite verb. For example:

Some consider diagramming sentences a waste of time.

Figure 4–6

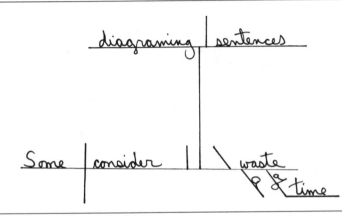

Nouns may be used as indirect objects or in other ways that Reed and Kellogg sensibly classify as adverbial and diagram as elliptical prepositional phrases. For example:

I sold him the wheat for a dollar a bushel.

Figure 4–7

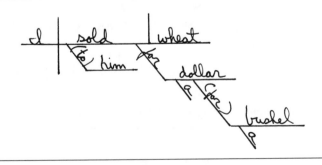

In contrast to traditionalists, modern theoretical linguistics has set the goal of describing the rules by which a computer could generate grammatical sentences. Every grammatical feature must be expressed as a choice among possible paths leading to a specific string of words. This effort has led to the development of "tree diagrams." Each tree diagram begins with an S, which stands for "sentence." The first rule of grammar is that every S bifurcates into an NP and a VP, a noun phrase and a verb phrase. Thereafter, possibilities multiply. All of them are presumably present in the mind of the speaker, but linguists only spell out the paths actually chosen in the creation of a given sentence. For example, an NP may consist of "det+adj+n," a determiner[52] plus an adjective plus a noun. The choices become more and more specific until you reach the actual string of words at the end.

Max Morenberg's *Doing Grammar* is a popular textbook containing a lucid explanation of tree diagrams with many examples. Whereas traditionalists like Reed and Kellogg draw examples from literature, Morenberg's aims at the immediate concerns of his students. Here is his diagram of the sentence, *Intense pressure from the drug counselor made the teenagers angry.*

Figure 4–8

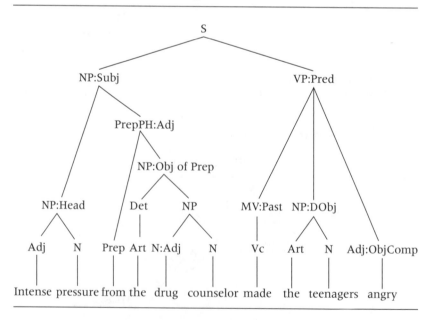

In a Reed and Kellogg diagram, the same sentence looks like this:

Figure 4–9

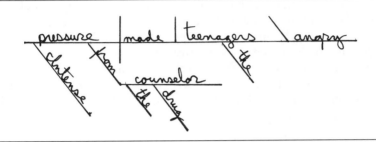

Both diagrams symbolize essentially the same information and presuppose a knowledge of the parts of speech. It seems evident to me that the Reed–Kellogg diagram is far more economical. In fact, I am still fuming over an email posting I once saw referring to traditional diagrams with "lines running off in all directions." For the benefit of the easily confused author of that message, there are exactly three kinds of lines in Reed—Kellogg diagrams: horizontal, vertical, and those at a forty-five-degree angle. This particular diagram involves ten separate strokes, the same as the number of words in the sentence. By way of contrast, the tree diagram involves twenty-nine different lines and seventeen labels.

Tree diagrams are especially suitable to sentences written in normal English word order. Because they assume the burden of yielding the final string of words exactly as spoken or written, even commonplace departures from the rule that subjects come first lead to complicated explanations. In the sentence *"There are millions of drug dealers in the United States,"* Morenberg describes *there* as the "grammatical subject." He diagrams *millions of drug dealers* as part of the predicate but calls it the "logical subject." The distinction is somewhat confusing, however. *Millions of drug dealers* functions as the grammatical subject, too, at least in the sense that it governs the form of the main verb: "there <u>are</u> millions of drug dealers," but "there <u>is</u> one drug dealer."

In contrast, traditional grammar does not attempt to explain every characteristic of sentences as actually written or spoken. Some features are relegated to the category of the idiomatic usage or poetic license

and not included in the representation of the sentence's basic structure. Attention is thus focused on features that all sentences have in
common. In the case of the drug-dealer sentence, *Millions etc.* would
be diagramed as the subject; *are,* as an intransitive verb (*be* used in its
"existential" sense of "exist"), and *there* as an adverb modifying *are.* Its
idiomatic use as an expletive or filler with the *be* in an existential sense
would be mentioned in a footnote.

Because they ignore word order, traditional diagrams are easily
applied to poetic sentences with artistic transpositions and to those in
various languages, including classical Greek and Latin in which word
order is extremely free. The examples below show how traditional diagrams illuminate the similarities in syntactical structure underlying
different languages.

1. *Omne tulit punctum qui miscuit utile dulci.* (Horace: "He who has
   mixed the useful with the sweet has won every vote.")

Figure 4–10

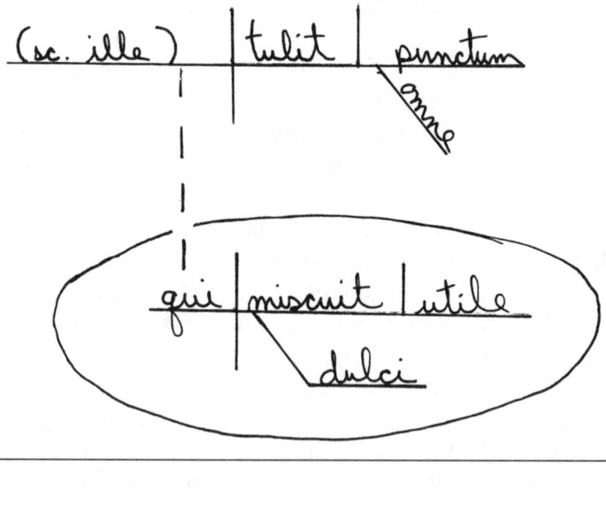

2. *Nel mezzo del cammin di nostra vita / Mi ritrovai per una selva oscura /
   Che la diritta via era smarrita.* (Dante: "In the middle of our life's
   path, I found myself in a dark wood where the direct way had
   been hidden.")

Figure 4–11

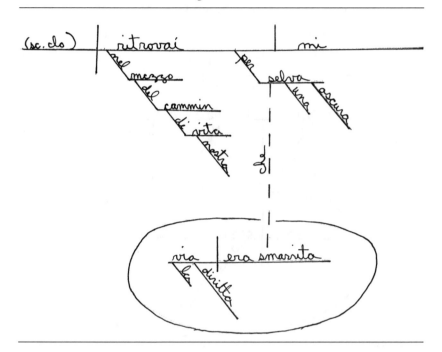

3. *Glücklich allein ist die Seele die liebt.* (Goethe: "Only the soul that loves is happy.")

Figure 4–12

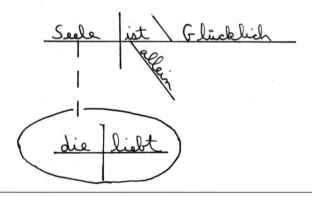

4. *Le coeur a ses raisons que la raison ne connait point.* (Pascal: "The heart has its reasons that reason does not know.")

Figure 4–13

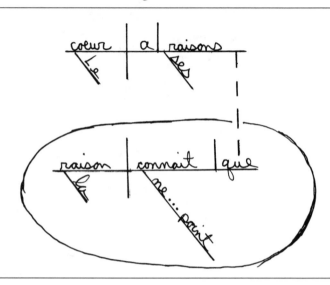

Traditional grammarians have always been intent on teaching students to understand particular languages, whereas the speculative grammarians of the middle ages and contemporary transformationalists and structuralists have aimed at describing a universal grammar. Ironically, it is the traditionalists whose system of diagramming can be most easily applied to a wide variety of languages.

Reed and Kellogg never attempted to impose sentence diagrams on anyone. In their introduction to *Higher Lessons,* they say that they themselves are convinced of the diagrams' utility, but that they do not form a "vital" part of the work and could be omitted without a break. They are presented as an aid to comprehension to those who wish to use them. Personally, I have used them extensively for decades in my teaching and research—with humble gratitude to Sister Catherine Albert who showed me how to do them back in the fourth grade. Very few of my Latin students have diagrammed sentences previously and are generally reluctant to try them on their own, but they do find diagrams helpful to consult and frequently ask me to use them in explicating difficult sentences. In my own research, I am often stymied by the meaning of a complicated sentence in ancient Greek or Latin or in scholarly articles in German. The problem is hardly ever a matter of vocabulary, since the meanings of individual words are readily available in dictionaries and can usually be guessed from context. Serious problems in comprehension are almost always matters of grammatical structure. Under those circumstances, I routinely resort to diagramming the sentences according to the Reed–Kellogg method. Normally, the obscurity vanishes before I finish the diagram. This experience has persuaded me that most students could improve their comprehension if they were schooled in sentence diagramming. In fact, though the practice is no longer common, it is far from being extinct, as many people assume. As just mentioned, they are featured in popular textbooks by Kolln and Lester. We will see below that they are used intensively in at least a few outstanding private schools.

As I revised this chapter, a good example of the utility of Reed and Kellogg's diagrams as an aid to interpretation fell into my lap. I happened to be preparing to participate in a roundtable discussion of a selection of Emily Dickinson's poems, including the popular 501, which goes in part:

> This World is not Conclusion,
>
> A Species stands beyond—
>
> Invisible, as Music—
>
> But positive as Sound . . .
>
> To guess it, puzzles scholars
>
> To gain it, men have borne
>
> Contempt of generations
>
> And Crucifixion, shown—. . . .
>
> Much Gesture, from the Pulpit
>
> Strong Hallelujahs roll—
>
> Narcotics cannot still the Tooth
>
> That nibbles at the soul—

Judging by my own experience, one's intuitive grasp of Dickinson's meaning is likely to fail at the line "And Crucifixion, shown." Baffled by this line, I resorted by old habit to diagramming the sentence. Since "shown" and "borne" are both past participles, it was natural to think that they were two limbs of a compound verbal phrase linked by *and*. The direct object of "borne" was "contempt of generations." "Crucifixion" could be assumed to represent the direct object of "shown." But "men have shown Crucifixion" seemed a pointlessly obscure way to say that men were crucified, if that indeed was its meaning. Hence, maybe some other element was understood by ellipsis. If so, it could only be "contempt of." In other words:

Figure 4–14

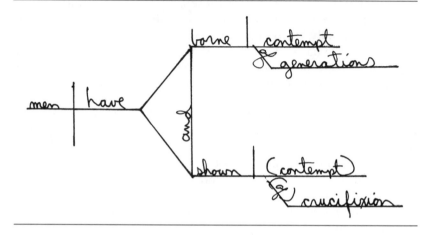

Once I saw this, it seemed so obvious that I began to doubt whether the sentence could be used, as it had occurred to me to do, as an example of the explanatory power of diagrams. Perhaps less obtuse readers understood this structure intuitively, instantly. This concern was allayed by my discovery that the lines were interpreted in two quite different and (I would maintain) mistaken ways in the first two recent books on Dickinson's poetry that I consulted.[53]

Notes

1. Ravitch, 99. My brief history of progressive education draws heavily on Ravitch's excellent work.

2. Two documents, cited by Ravitch, 41–47 and 123–27, epitomize the conversion of the teaching profession to a progressive outlook. These are descriptions of the ideal goals of secondary education published by the National Education Association (NEA) in 1893 and 1918, respectively. The committee that issued the 1893 statement was chaired by Harvard President Charles Eliot. Although it advocated liberalizing the curriculum—e.g., by giving the study of modern languages the same status as the study of Latin—it favored the same academic curriculum for all students and was, therefore, criticized by progressives for trying to impose a college education on everyone. The 1918 document took these criticisms to heart. It was published by the NEA's Commission on the Reorganization of Secondary Education (CRSE) and was chaired by the supervisor of high schools in Massachusetts. The CRSE listed the main goals of secondary education as: "1. health, 2. command of fundamental processes, 3. worthy home membership, 4. vocation, 5. citizenship, 6. worthy use of leisure, 7. ethical character." Of these, only the second

item, command of fundamental processes, refers to traditional academic skills. In practical terms, the proposed reorganization of secondary education entails a drastic reduction of emphasis on the liberal arts.

3. John of Salisbury, I.24 (67–68).

4. Dewey, 11.

5. The questions are taken from a booklet available at the Library of Congress: *Eighth Grade Examination Question Book, All the Questions Issued for Eighth Grade Examinations by the State Superintendents of Public Instruction of Nebraska, since January 1st, 1915.* Compiled by Sam C. Stephenson, 1921.

6. Dewey, 10.

7. Cremin, 295–98.

8. The evolution of instruction in grammar in the Winnetka public schools is interesting. It is reported in a book published in 1962, *Winnetka: The History and Significance of an Educational Experiment.* Washburne wrote the first half of the book, giving the history of the system from its beginning until 1943. The second part was written by Sidney P. Marland, who became superintendent in 1956 after brief tenures by four others. Marland's portion of the book reports on the evolution of grammar and usage: "For a time, the Winnetka Schools deferred the teaching of formal grammar to Grade VIII, with the belief…that the mechanics of our language could be rather quickly and efficiently mastered in a short while at Grade VIII, avoiding the inefficient and time-consuming struggle at an earlier age. Evidence has unfolded over the years, indicating that the heavy expectations for grammar and usage at Grade VIII, accumulated by 'deferral,' were so demanding that (a) they were not wholly mastered in the year, and (b) much other important work in Grade VIII language arts…had to be curtailed. Accordingly, we have spread the teaching of grammar and usage over all the upper grades, starting at Grade III." Marland includes the school district's official lists of goals for the fourth grade in the area of grammar and usage from 1944 and 1961, respectively. The 1944 list has eight topics, mostly having to do with capitalization. By 1961, the list has grown to twenty-eight and includes such concepts as declarative, interrogative, and exclamatory sentences, and "nouns: number, gender, as subject; verbs: action and being, as predicate." Topics to be "previewed" include "Nouns: proper, common, possessive; adjectives: recognition, modifiers of nouns and pronouns; pronouns: recognition, number, gender, used as subject." The Winnetka curriculum shows that the study of grammar is not antithetical to the spirit of moderate progressive education, which recognizes the importance of formal knowledge. Reasonable progressive educators merely want to ensure that students are given ample opportunity to exercise reflective judgments as well as being drilled on essential determinate ones, not to exclude the latter.

9. Kilpatrick, 317.

10. Cremin, 149.

11. Bobbitt, 241.

12. Bobbitt, 247–48.

13. Bobbitt, 249.

14. Fries, 5.

15. Fries, 9.

16. Fries, 17.

17. Aristotle, *Peri Hermeneias* ("On Interpretation"), 16a (my translation).

18. Pinker, 117.

19. Most qualms had to do with elliptical sentences, which are obvious to people but not to computers. Consider this exchange:

> "Who killed Caesar?"

> "Brutus."

Brutus can be described as a complete sentence because the words *killed Caesar* are inferred from the context, yet the single word *Brutus* obviously does not have any empirical qualities that make it a sentence.

It may be true that the traditional definition of a sentence as the expression of a "complete thought" is too ambiguous, although it is not an unreasonable way to refer in one brief phrase to a proposition, question, or command. When thus explained, the complete-thought definition is certainly not difficult to comprehend or to apply. Students who have problems distinguishing complete sentences from fragments never have difficulty recognizing questions or commands. Problems lie in distinguishing declarative sentences from fragments. In my experience, the Aristotelian test—i.e., a declarative sentence could be judged true or false—quickly clears up confusion in this area, even for students who understand little else about grammar.

20. Fries, 67.

21. Priestley, 6.

22. Chomsky, 1985, 2.

23. Davis, 162.

24. Davis, 165.

25. Hillocks and Smith, 596.

26. Elley (1976), 9.

27. Elley (1976), 17.

28. Macauley, 153.

29. Macauley, 162.

30. Hillocks and Smith, 591.

31. Hirsch, 71.

32. Caxton, 26–27.

33. Pinker, 28.

34. Pinker, 373–374.

35. Hook, 207.

36. Lowth, 16–17. He seems to be right. Greek has a definite article, similar in meaning and use to *the* in English. "Unto the death" would have been *achri tou thanatou*.

37. Lowth, 127–28.

38. Lowth, 107.

39. Alford, 188.

40. Visser (ii) 1035–39.

41. Although Alford's rule was mistaken, it did somehow become a clichéd symbol of excessively careful speech. As far as I can ascertain, however, it has not been defended by serious grammarians. Indeed, an arch prescriptivist, Henry Fowler, went to great lengths to discredit it in his 1926 classic *Modern English Usage*. "We maintain," he wrote, "that a real split infinitive, though not desirable in itself, is preferable to either of two things, to real ambiguity, and to patent artificiality. For the first, we will rather write 'Our object is to further cement trade relations' than, by correcting into "Our object is further to cement . . .', leave it doubtful whether an additional object or additional cementing is the point. And for the second, we take it that such reminders of a tyrannous convention as 'in not combining to forbid flatly hostilities' are far more abnormal than the abnormality they evade."

42. Pinker, 191–92. He invokes principles from transformational grammar to argue that prepositions with compound objects do not necessarily govern the case of both of their objects and concludes that a language with a rule enforcing such governance "is not a possible human language," which would seem to exclude Latin and Greek from the category of possible human languages. But I may misunderstand his argument.

43. This is the line taken, for example, by David Foster Wallace in his essay cited in Chapter One.

44. Hirsch, 72.

45. Watson, 20.

46. Watson, 58.

47. Pinker, 88.

48. Reed and Kellogg, 1987, 7.

49. Hunt, 167–68.

50. Reed and Kellogg, 1987, 9.

51. Reed and Kellogg placed object complements to the left of direct objects: *truth / shall make / free you*. One of Kolln's (1982) revisions in the system was to put object complements on the right of direct objects, thus staying closer to normal word order. I have incorporated this revision, as did Lester (1990).

52. On "determiners," see note 14 in Chapter Two.

53. James McIntosh, *Nimble Believing: Dickinson and the Unknown* (Ann Arbor: University of Michigan Press: 2000), p. 33, summarizes their meaning thus: "She expresses...respect for the 'Men'—the Christian martyrs and others like them—who have 'shown Crucifixion' to gain heaven." For a third interpretation, see Cynthia G. Wolff, *Emily Dickinson* (New York: Alfred A. Knopf, 1986), p. 269.

Chapter Five

Grammar at the Dawn of the Third Millennium

Where Are Despots When You Really Need One?

In recent years, the study of grammar has been making a comeback, but pitfalls remain. The most encouraging developments have occurred in England. I have focused on the decline of grammar in the United States since the sixties. If I had considered Great Britain instead, the story would have been much the same until 1998. In that year, Britain's New Labour government made grammatical analysis the central point of its National Literacy Strategy, an integrated syllabus for teaching reading and writing in England's primary schools—i.e., for five- to eleven-year-olds. In December of 1999, inspectors from the Office of Standards in Education[1] concluded that teachers' poor knowledge of grammar and punctuation had contributed to problems in teaching writing. In response, Education Secretary David Blunkett, who is spearheading the campaign to revive grammar, distributed a 216-page guide on teaching grammar to all primary schools and provided funding for all fifth- and sixth-grade teachers to attend one day of training on the new material. The goals emphasize a conceptual understanding of grammar. An example cited by Blunkett was that "10-year-olds should be able to discuss how changes from the active to the passive affect word order and sense of the sentence."[2]

This attempt to revive the study of grammar by governmental fiat is reminiscent of King Henry VIII's imposition of Lily's grammar on the schools of Shakespeare's day. The current opposition to and ignorance of traditional grammar is firmly entrenched, however. It may not be possible to transform education in the language arts so quickly. Nevertheless, events in Britain should be watched. If the reform has the desired effect, it will be a compelling argument for a similar effort in the United States.

The U.S. Standards Movement

In this country, much of the desire to improve education has been channeled into the development of new academic standards. The reader will recall that my brief involvement in formulating Wisconsin's new academic standards led to the writing of this book. I have subsequently come to believe that these standards are more of a problem than a solution in the area of the language arts.

The call for national standards came from an education summit of the nation's governors held in Charlottesville, Virginia, in 1989 at the invitation of President George H. W. Bush. In 1991 and 1992, the Department of Education responded by awarding grants to organizations to develop standards in seven subjects (science, history, geography, the arts, civics, foreign language, and English). In 1994, President Bill Clinton's first major education legislation, "Goals 2000," provided funds for states to develop standards of their own. Of critical importance, however, is the fact that National Council of Teachers of Mathematics (NCTM), acting independently, promulgated its own standards, which were published in 1989. In the early 1990s, the NCTM math standards seemed to be enjoying great success and were used as a model for the other standards.[3]

The mathematics standards introduced terminology and a method of organization that have become universal in the standards movements. They define the ideal mathematics curriculum by establishing "content standards" and "performance standards" to be met by students at various points along the way. Content standards denote areas of study; performance standards describe tasks that students should be able to perform under the rubric of each content standard. For example, under the content standard, "properties of numbers," eighth grade students are expected to be able to solve real-world problems involving fractions, ratios, proportions, and percentages. The latter are "performance standards."

A shortcoming of the original NCTM standards was that they omitted the mastery of basic skills. Rather than stipulating that students be able to meet performance standards by themselves, they recommended the use of calculators from the earliest grades. This feature of the NCTM standards provoked a backlash in 1995 starting with a group of parents and educators in California, who called themselves

"Mathematically Correct." Thanks to them, the omission of basic skills in the NCTM standards has been robustly criticized, and efforts of have been made to avoid the same pitfall in the development of standards for other subjects.

In contrast, the use of "content standards" and "performance standards" has become universal in the standards movement. The underlying idea that academic subjects should be viewed as training that will issue in a certain number of real-world performances has a long history in progressive education. An early exponent is Franklin Bobbitt, whose work from the 1920s has been cited above and whose lists of curricular objectives bear an unmistakable family resemblance to the academic standards of the nineties.[4]

Performance standards make sense in the domain of mathematics, but in English and other humanistic disciplines they become a strange Procrustean bed. Mathematics is a uniquely determinate discipline. Generally speaking, mathematical problems have one correct answer, which is obtained by rigid adherence to a set of explicit rules. These qualities make it possible for calculators to do virtually everything that students are asked to do in math classes. The various subdivisions of mathematics clearly correspond to different kinds of performances by which mastery is demonstrated. I can show that I understand a certain amount of plane geometry by computing the area of a circle on the basis of its diameter.

The relationship between content and performance is radically different in the language arts and, indeed, in the other humanities. As one advances in these disciplines, reflective judgments become progressively more important. There is great latitude for free choice. They do not issue in performances of particular types that can be described ahead of time. Instead, they pervade our thoughts and actions, benefiting us in ways that cannot be foreseen. When we do give "performances" involving our abilities in the language arts or other humanistic disciplines, there is some relationship between the specific things that we have learned and the quality of our performance, but this relationship is impossible to quantify.

The absurdity of applying content and performance standards to the language arts is most apparent in the study of literature. It is eminently reasonable to suggest that young students should read some unquestionably great and yet accessible works of literature—e.g., *The Odyssey, Macbeth, Huckleberry Finn*. In the real world, however, reading a classic does not result in a "performance." The authors of our standards, however, are obliged by their own ground rules to pretend that it does. In Wisconsin's standards, which are typical in this regard, they end up treating literary criticism as the performance standard that corresponds to the content standard of reading serious literature. In reality, of course, literary criticism is the province of mature, professional scholars, and even in their hands its value is not always obvious. The approach results in performance standards that would place absurdly high expectations on a student, if they were taken seriously. For example, according to Wisconsin's standards, twelfth grade students are expected to:

Read, interpret and critically analyze literature.

Explain the structure of selected classical and contemporary works of literature, in whole and in part, from various cultures and historical periods, and illustrate ways in which authors use syntax, imagery, figures of speech, allusion, symbols, irony, and other devices in the context of history, culture, and style.

Draw on a broad base of knowledge about the universal themes of literature such as initiation, love and duty, heroism, illusion and reality, salvation, death and rebirth, and explain how these themes are developed in a particular work of literature.

Investigate and report on ways in which a writer has influenced or been influenced by historical, social, and cultural issues or events.

Develop, explain, and defend interpretations of complex literary works.

Explain how details of language, setting, plot, character, conflict, point of view, and voice in a work of literature combine to produce a dominant tone, effect or theme.

Develop and apply criteria to evaluate the literary merit of unfamiliar works.[5]

Obviously, performance standards like these will never be applied with any rigor. No high school senior will ever be relegated to summer school until he comes up with a compelling analysis of the relationship between ancient Athenian constitutional history and Sophocles' *Antigone*, for example. If such standards are to be enforced at all, students would be well-advised to skip the reading of the primary texts and to go directly to summaries and secondary sources so that they can imitate professional critics.

The underlying problem is that the benefits of reading a great book pervade our lives, but they do not naturally issue in any one real-world performance that demonstrates mastery of that book. I have taught literature courses on the college level for many years. The experience has left me absolutely certain of two facts. First, reading classical works with comprehension is generally beneficial to young minds. Second, the only reliable way to induce students to read such works and to ascertain whether they actually did so is to ask them questions about the content of the work—not about possible interpretations. For example, just before he returns to battle in *The Iliad*, Achilles hears a prophecy of his own death from an unusual, nonhuman source. What is it? Students who have read the book with attention are very likely to remember the correct answer, his horse. Those who have not are not likely to guess it correctly.

I am fully aware that as a real-world performance, answering such objective questions about the content of a work of literature has no practical value. That is not the point. The point is that reading the book with attention has a value that pervades one's life in ways that cannot be measured by educators and that objective questions are the only practical way to induce students to do so and ascertain whether they did.

The situation with literature is typical of the language arts and other humanistic disciplines. The knowledge acquired in various "content" areas does not issue in particular performances. As a practical matter, therefore, it needs to be measured directly by "objective" testing. Humanities classes should, of course, contain ample time for the free-wheeling exploration and application of humanistic knowledge. In the case of classical literature, discussions in which students are genuinely free to raise their own questions and express their own reactions, rather than imitating academic critics, are extremely valuable and often life-altering experiences. Nevertheless, if we want to make sure that our students have actually read a classic, we have to be willing to ask them, at some point, what happens on its pages.

The same kind of observations apply to the study of grammar and vocabulary. Conscious knowledge of the nature of the sentence, the parts of speech, the conjugation of verbs, and the meanings of individual words enhances our ability to use and comprehend language pervasively. It does not correspond directly to particular kinds of performance. In the case of grammar, the commitment of standards writers to performances has led them to focus on subdivisions of grammar that affect what are called the "mechanics of writing." For example, in Wisconsin's standards, it is mandated that fourth grade students will "use punctuation marks and conjunctions, as appropriate, to separate sentences and connect independent clause." There is no requirement that students be able to explain what a sentence is and how it differs from a dependent clause. The implication is that sentences and dependent clauses may be recognized "intuitively." Only the performance counts. In this way, the use of content and performance standards guarantees that the radically progressive approach to grammar, with its exclusive interest in avoiding "mechanical errors" and its minimal emphasis on conceptual understanding, will continue to dominate.

Whereas the standards approach results in minimizing the importance of grammar, it leads to the setting of exalted goals for writing in general. The Wisconsin Language Arts standards are typical in this respect. They envision classrooms in which every student is a prolific author as well as an erudite literary critic. One of its performance standards under the content standard of writing requires that by the end of grade 12 every student will:

> Write creative fiction that includes an authentic setting, discernible tone, coherent plot, distinct characters, effective detail, believable dialogue, and reasonable resolution of conflict.[6]

This is a description of a publishable work of fiction. We might as well say that no students will graduate from high school in Wisconsin without publishing at least one story in the *Kenyon Review.*

In the real world, competence in English is a pervasive advantage, but it does not often result in a steady stream of short stories, novels, poems, plays, TV scripts, and treatises. It is a kind of understanding that needs to be measured directly, not because the mere possession of this knowledge in a static form is valuable in and of itself, but because its value is too pervasive and subtle to be demonstrated by particular performances. Obviously, students should be given many opportunities to use their knowledge of language creatively. Furthermore, it is reasonable to require competent performances in some basic kinds of writing that do not require special inspiration—e.g., business letters and expository essays. It can only be counterproductive, however, to pretend that students of the future will not be allowed to graduate unless they have produced a series of inspired creations in different literary genres. Standards that are cast at such a high level will be ignored and quickly forgotten. Instead, students' understanding of language must be assessed directly. Minister Blunkett's notion that "10-year-olds should be able to discuss how changes from the active to the passive affect word order and sense of the sentence" illustrates exactly the kind of standard that is needed.

Oases of Humanism

When I first started to reflect on my students' deficient training in grammar, I thought that everyone would agree that a firm grasp of basic grammatical concepts, typified by the parts of speech, was an important part of a good elementary education. After a year of research, I was beginning to think that the opposite was true, that nobody except me still clung to this strange belief. Now I know that I am in a minority, at least among teachers, but not entirely alone. I have already mentioned the current British government as one ally. In order to end on a positive note, I would like to mention four others.

I have already cited one of them, the Elm Grove Lutheran School in the Milwaukee suburbs. Here students in the seventh and eighth grades are given solid, formal instruction in grammar by Paul Greutzmacher, a teacher with a legion of admirers who attest to the value of his teaching in their later lives. Researchers who are looking for empirical evidence of the effects of formal instruction in grammar ought to follow the careers of students from programs like Greutzmacher's rather than testing the short-term effects of grammar lessons that they themselves devise.

One of the many things that has endeared Greutzmacher to his students is his creation of a game known as "verb tense football." Having observed it being played just once, I can give only a general impression of the rules. Students call for a run, a pass, or a kick and then must produce a given person, number, and tense of a verb, typically an obscure one, in ten seconds. If they succeed, their team advances its position on a chalkboard field. For example:

Player one: "Pass play."

Opponent: "Future perfect progressive, first person plural."

Referee: "To resurrect."

Player one: "We will have been resurrecting."

Referee: "Correct. Advance the ball fifteen yards. First down."

Of course, there are a number of detailed rules governing kick returns, points after touchdowns, and so on. On the day that I observed, four games were played simultaneously. All the students were absorbed and knew the rules so well that their communications were rapid and elliptical. It was like watching the floor of a stock exchange on a busy day. Most of the games were close and not settled until the last verb. Such contests are held annually around the time of the Super Bowl. The result is that terms like "future progressive," which befuddle most contemporary collegians, are second nature to Greutzmacher's students. But I mention "verb tense football" chiefly because it is the most dramatic refutation that I have seen of the notion that grammar classes are necessarily dull.

Another set of students whom researchers would be well-advised to study are graduates of the Independence School in Newark, Delaware. A K–8 school, Independence, was founded in 1978 and has enjoyed remarkable success. It has doubled in size since its founding, now enrolls more than 700 students, and continues to grow. Independence's original headmaster, Ken Weinig, still at the helm, is a thoughtful, articulate educator. One of his guiding principles is that gifted students need structure in education at least as much as do average students. He likes to make the point that "one can have an IQ of 150 and still be lazy." When asked for evidence of the academic effectiveness of the Independence curriculum, he said that he traced the high school careers of forty-two Independence students from the eighth grade class of 1991. The highlight of their generally satisfactory performances was that six of them went on to become high school valedictorians.

Weinig is the most emphatic advocate of sentence diagramming that I have met. It is the backbone of instruction in grammar that Independence students receive from third through eighth grades. Weinig believes that diagrams are especially helpful to students whose verbal abilities lag, since they appeal to the right side of the brain. He reports observing some such students diagramming sentences correctly before they are able to name their constituent parts.

Weinig provided me with the names of some of the high schools that Independence graduates attend. I wrote to one of them, The Archmere Academy, a prestigious, private, college preparatory school, asking for a characterization of the writing abilities of students coming out of Independence. Daniel Hickey, the director of Admissions and a freshman English teacher, kindly wrote back, saying,

> I have found that the Independence students are at a distinct advantage [in Freshman English] already being familiar with grammatical principles and seem to more quickly assimilate them into their writing than do the students who have not been as well prepared. Their writing, as a whole, strikes me as more polished and deliberate. . . . In my experience it has been more difficult to teach writing to the students that don't have the strong grammar foundation that the students from the Independence School enjoy.

In evaluating Mr. Hickey's testimony, it should be noted that he is comparing the performance of Independence students against others attending his exclusive prep school. If the progressive critique of formal instruction in grammar were valid, Independence students would surely show the negative effects of all those hours wasted in diagramming sentences.

The nation's best known oasis of formal instruction in grammar is the Calvert School in Baltimore, Maryland. This is an independent, pre-K–8 school with a competitive admissions policy and rigorous academic standards. Students are trained in a standard handwriting script and produce copious essays, which they are required to correct until they are perfect. In addition, they receive thorough formal instruction in grammar in the early grades. Reed–Kellogg style diagrams are used extensively. Calvert enjoys an excellent reputation and has become one of the nation's leading producers of materials for home schooling, which include books on grammar. Attempts have been made to transport the Calvert curriculum into public schools in Baltimore. Although they have enjoyed some success, the need to accept transfer students in public schools and to prepare for state-mandated, standardized tests has made it difficult to maintain the integrity of the Calvert curriculum.

Calvert's lessons in formal grammar are thorough, systematic, and carefully graduated. In the fourth grade, students are introduced to the parts of speech, the conjugation of verbs, and the structure of sentences, but they do not receive a separate grade in grammar. In the fifth and sixth grades, grammar becomes a separately graded subject. Simplified terminology—e.g., "past tense with a helper"—is gradually replaced with the mature equivalents—e.g., "past participle." Even in the sixth grade, exposition stays at a fairly rudimentary level. Students diagram simple and compound sentences but do not tackle ones with subordinate clauses, infinitives, or participles. The final exam in sixth grade grammar that I was shown concluded with ten sentences to diagram, of which the most challenging were compounded ones—e.g., "The very little child cried and cried, and his mother finally came." Calvert's home-schooling materials in grammar continue through the eighth grade and include diagramming complex sentences, infinitives, gerunds, and participles.

It would be unfair to suggest that public schools are lax because they do not usually rise to the standards maintained by a Calvert or that the excellence of Calvert's students results exclusively from formal instruction in grammar. On the other hand, formal instruction in grammar is an integral part of what any reasonable person would acknowledge to be a highly successful language arts curriculum. Forced at a tender age to memorize the definitions of parts of speech and even to diagram sentences, Calvert students should be, according to the dominant theory, stilted and self-conscious when given the opportunity to express themselves freely. The opposite is the case. Calvert faculty members take special pride in their student compositions, whose excellence they attribute in large part to their thorough grounding in grammar. What struck me in the Calvert student compositions that I read were the qualities of wit and uninhibited imagination. The sense is palpable that the young authors can capture random thoughts and images precisely because they are in conscious control of the formal elements of their medium. Nothing does more for creativity than self-confidence, and nothing does more for self-confidence than conscious understanding.

To exemplify, I quote from Calvert's *Silhouettes 2000*, an annual anthology of student writing. My selections are ones that struck me as being particularly amusing, but they are by no means atypical. And it should be noted that the stories display not only lively imaginations, but also an ostentatious mastery of punctuation. This should not be surprising since Calvert teachers do not accept papers with so much as a misplaced comma. In fact, their practice runs directly counter to the conventional wisdom in schools of education that teachers should not harp on the avoidance of little errors. Calvert has policy of zero tolerance for errors of any kind in grammar, spelling, or punctuation. Far from inhibiting young writers, this approach seems to embolden them. My first exhibit is by a ten-year-old, Margaret Comer: "Jelly Jars Come Alive!"

> On April 3rd, 4012, a computer glitch at the Jupiter Jams factory made two jars of jelly come alive. One was a jar of mint jam and the other was of peach. This scene is set in the Jupiter Jams factory.
> "Hey! I'm alive! I'm the only one alive in this whole factory!" said Mint.
> "You wish," someone behind him exclaimed.
> Mint said, "Oh, hi, Peach. I knew this was too good to last."
> "Well, I've been thinking," started Peach.
> "What? What?" interrupted Mint.
> "Don't interrupt!" Peach snapped. "As I was saying we're going to have to stick together—as in teamwork. I'll be the management and you be the labor." (p. 73)

Female authors dominate the pages of *Silhouettes*. The development of literary finesse seems to be a greater challenge for the males, but even among them there are examples of outstanding promise, as in "The Dreadfully Late Day," by eleven-year-old Mike Prebil:

> I heard my alarm clock sound. I glanced up and noticed I woke up late! When I opened my eyes, I saw my hamster, Kobe, on my chin. I let out a surprised yelp, and my hamster, who was equally alarmed, slipped and fell right into my mouth! I reached into my mouth and pulled the squirming hamster out. I stood up and tossed my blanket back on my bed. While I was walking away, I noticed a few unsanitary presents my hamster had left me overnight. I had the distinct feeling that my hamster was laughing at me. (p. 80)

Silhouettes's poetry is also impressive. I am particularly fond of a piece by ten-year-old Dani Perez's, "Last Night":

> Last night I wished up a star
>
> And wished that I had wings.
>
> A fairy had to sew them on.
>
> But now it really stings! (p. 60)

Nearer to my home, The Brookfield Academy, in Brookfield, Wisconsin, a suburb of Milwaukee, is a K–12 school, whose language arts curriculum emphasizes formal instruction in traditional grammar and sentence diagramming in grades four through six. As in the case of the Calvert School, the Brookfield faculty relies on material that they produce themselves. It consists of a straightforward exposition of grammatical concepts illustrated by diagrams. The Brookfield Academy is also a relatively expensive and selective school, though not to the same degree as Calvert. The value of the evidence that it provides is of the same nature. Formal instruction in traditional grammar is a central feature of an obviously successful language arts curriculum. The verbal SAT scores of Brookfield graduates in 1999 were eighty-six points above the national average.

The Brookfield experience also belies the belief that grammar is an essentially boring subject that will alienate and discourage the students who are forced to study it. On the contrary, the teachers report that it is a popular subject. I have visited their classes and found this characterization to be undeniably true. One fifth grade class enjoys a game in which they are allowed to realize abstract diagrams with "gross" sentences. When I challenged them to produce a "gross" linking sentence whose subject was a gerund with a direct object, every hand in the class shot up. The first response: "Spewing chunks is unpleasant."

The experiences of teachers at schools like Calvert and the Brookfield Academy show that there is no reason that grammatical concepts cannot be taught slowly, carefully, and systematically to young students. The results of doing so are that the students acquire a conscious understanding of the structures of their own language. They take understandable pride in this achievement and enjoy increased self-confidence and creativity in expressing themselves. They are ready to do great things in the language arts.

Brief Concluding Remarks

Learning grammar taught me how to think—to pay attention to the neat and precise relationships between things, to look for subtle differences, to grapple with complexity. I always felt as if a world of logic resided in my grammar lessons, and when I got to high school English classes, even classes on novels, plays, and short stories, I was leaps and bounds ahead of students who had never had the same chance to study grammar.

—Danielle Allen[7]

I do not argue that formal instruction in grammar in the early grades is a panacea for the problems faced by our nation's schools, but I do believe that it would be an important step in the right direction. I recognize that it is hard to teach traditional grammar to children who do not speak standard English at home. I also acknowledge the staggering difficulties encountered generally by teachers in low-income areas. Problems of either kind may well alter pedagogical pace and methods, but letting such problems change the *goals* of education is a way of surrendering to them.

Understanding of grammar has declined across the board. Nothing would do more to improve American students' knowledge of grammar than taking steps to ensure that K–12 teachers themselves understand basic concepts. State standards calling for more emphasis on grammar in the K–12 curriculum will not be effective unless the teachers are well-prepared.

Requirements for certification in teaching English vary from state to state. They are, however, subjected to some control. Roughly half of the nation's programs for certifying teachers are accredited by the National Council for Accreditation of Teacher Education (NCATE). In the area of language arts, the NCATE relies on guidelines produced every ten years by the NCTE. The latest version of the NCTE guidelines appeared in 1996 in the form of a 72-page booklet. At the heart of the booklet are chapters on the attitudes, knowledge, and pedagogical techniques needed by "effective language arts teachers." The NCTE distilled fifty-nine specific "standards" from these chapters. Teacher programs in the language arts must give the NCATE evidence that they are living up to each of these standards in order to be accredited by them.

None of the standards is hard-edged. Typical is the requirement that teachers be trained to "help students develop lifelong habits of critical thinking and judging." It is hard to imagine a program whose advocates could not make a case for its efforts in this direction.

The only reference to grammar in the NCTE guidelines runs as follows:

> Teachers should understand the significance of grammar systems as one way to discuss language, and they should understand the relationship of scholarly grammar systems to the production of language. This emphasis in instruction, however, should be based on the use of language rather than on an abstract study of it. Teachers need to provide opportunities for students to use non-academic as well as academic English. In doing so, they can help students understand when to use formal structures and when informal structures are appropriate. Teachers also must understand that the meaning and function of grammars are grounded in language, rather than thinking that grammar systems drive language.[8]

If we want teachers who understand grammar, more is needed. As we have seen, the word "grammar" is used in at least two different ways. It refers (1) to rules, deep-seated in the brain, that enable people, alone among God's creatures, to use language and (2) to relatively superficial, debatable rules defended by Pinker's "schoolmarms" and "language mavens"—e.g., the injunction against splitting infinitives. In this critical NCTE document, "grammar" is implicitly limited to the latter meaning. The gist of the guideline is that prospective teachers should be trained to keep this kind of grammar in a proper perspective, realizing that it is just one way to discuss language, that it is unnecessary for the production of language, that there are times when it is appropriate to disregard it, and that it is not the engine that drives language.

The standard distilled from this paragraph is quite ambiguous: prospective teachers should "demonstrate an understanding of English grammars." Only professional linguists master the "grammars" of several dialects of English—e.g., being able to conjugate verbs *à la* Chaucer, Black English Vernacular, Appalachian, and so forth. Since the standard is derived from the guideline just quoted, it is probably intended to mean that prospective teachers should be able to demonstrate a grasp of the fact that rules of usage vary from speaker to speaker and situation to situation. In any event, the effect of the current guidelines is to make it possible for prospective language arts teachers to be certified by NCATE-accredited schools without detailed knowledge of traditional grammar in the more fundamental sense. Needed are requirements making it perfectly clear that prospective teachers must master the fundamental concepts. They should be able to parse English sentences. They should know the parts of speech and be able to describe verbs correctly, giving person, number, tense, and voice, when they are finite, and identifying participles, infinitives, and gerunds as such. They should be able to analyze sentences into subjects and predicates and be able to distinguish the main clause in a sentence from subordinate clauses. The understanding of these concepts has little to do with the excessively nice prescriptions of language mavens. It helps people interpret the statements of others and express their own thoughts by giving them a firm grasp of the structural dimension of language.

Fundamental grammatical concepts are nearly mathematical in the precision of their application. The understanding of them is easy to demonstrate via determinate judgments—e.g., "In this sentence, that word is an adjective; that word is the main verb in the past progressive tense," or "In the first sentence of the Declaration of Independence, 'a due respect to the opinions of mankind' is the subject." The ability to make such judgments does not qualify a person to teach English any more than knowing the multiplication tables makes one a good math teacher. Attention must also be paid to developing the reflective abilities of prospective teachers. Nevertheless, an English teacher who does not know the parts of speech has the same kind of deficiency as a math teacher who does not know the product of eight times seven. We need teachers who understand basic grammatical concepts and who are committed to transmitting this understanding to their students soon after the students have learned how to read.

My emphasis on the value of tradition and on the analogy between the medieval modistae and contemporary linguists might leave the impression that I am opposed to change and progress in the study of language. In fact, I am happy to acknowledge the accomplishments of cutting-edge linguists and the fact that they can be helpful to teachers. In their day, the modistae themselves made valuable contributions. The notion of transitive verbs, for example, is derived from their work. Modern linguists have many similar accomplishments. For example, they have drawn attention to the fact that parts of speech are determined rather more by the formal characteristics of words than by their meanings. What makes *go* a verb is not so much that it denotes an action, as that it may take the suffix *-ing* and can follow a modal auxiliary. It is all to the good when teachers internalize and use such insights to revitalize their teaching.

There is, however, a difference between pedagogy and research. The liberal arts refer to humble, rudimentary skills: reading, writing, arithmetic. What they require are teachers who are willing to devote themselves to the transmission of very basic ideas, such as the parts of speech and the tenses of verbs. Cambridge University has just published a new grammar of the English language that runs to nearly two thousand pages.[9] Its authors claim *inter alia* that they have overthrown the traditional concept of the preposition.[10] There is, they say, no difference between the *in* in "Come in!", traditionally an adverb, and the *in* in "He came in a Chevrolet," a so-called preposition. At least one learned reviewer has taken issue with their analysis.[11] The argument is impossible for nonspecialists to follow. Meanwhile third- and fourth-graders are embarking on the study of English. I have observed that individuals who understand grammar well often memorized lists of prepositions, traditionally defined, as youngsters. This is valuable because it helps people identify the grammatical nuclei of sentences by first eliminating prepositional phrases. Characteristic of my point of view is the belief that it remains a good idea for young students to memorize such lists, despite the new Cambridge grammar and without impugning its scholarly value. My general point is that young students do not need the kind of understanding that contemporary linguists finally acquire at the ends of their careers. Young students need the kind of understanding that the linguists themselves started with when they were young. In most cases, that means a small number of broad concepts not so terribly different from what Shakespeare learned from Lily. We must guard against the mistake made in the high middle ages and skewered by Erasmus: undermining pedagogy by making a fetish of the latest theories. This can only confuse "young and tender wits."

Sentences always have and always will consist of clauses with subjects and predicates and of words that fall into classes fairly well described as verbs, nouns, adjectives, adverbs, pronouns, prepositions, conjunctions, and interjections. Individuals who understand these concepts have a distinct advantage over others where the use of language is involved—and that means everywhere. If only for the purpose of helping disadvantaged students, it should therefore be a high priority for all English teachers to find ways to deliver effective formal instruction in grammar in the middle grades of all schools, not just elite ones. There is reason to believe that this change of policy would also increase our nation's appreciation of its literary heritage, promote the study of foreign language, and improve the quality of the spoken and written discourse in which we are all immersed.

Notes

1. *London Times Educational Supplement,* Dec. 17, 1999.

2. "David Blunkett launches new grammar guide as literacy and numeracy gets further funding," *M2 Communications Ltd. M2 PRESSWIRE,* Sept. 20, 2000.

3. Ravitch, 432–33.

4. Cremin, 199, explains that Bobbitt's work grew out of his association with the NEA's Committee on Economy of Time in Education, which was charged with making recommendations for eliminating waste from the school curriculum.

5. Wisconsin Model Academic Standards, English Language Arts, Content Standard A (Reading/Literature), 12.2.

6. Wisconsin Model Academic Standards, English Language Arts, Content Standard B (Writing), 12.1: Create or produce writing to communicate with different audiences for a variety of purposes. Students are also required to produce effective argumentative writings, reflective writings, summaries of complex information, autobiographical and biographical narratives "in a mature style," and technical writings.

7. Allen, an African-American, is one of the nation's most distinguished, young intellectuals. She graduated summa cum laude in Classics from Princeton University in 1993, has earned master's and doctoral degrees in Classics from Cambridge University and master's and doctoral degrees in political theory from Harvard University. She has a long list of publications and has won numerous honors and awards, including one for original

poetry and a MacArthur "genius" award. She is currently an associate professor with joint appointments in the Department of Classical Languages and Literatures, the Department of Politics, and the Committee on Social Thought at the University of Chicago.

8. Small, 16.

9. Huddleston and Pullum, 2002.

10. Huddleston and Pullum, 2003.

11. Cp. Joybrato Mukherjee, LINGUIST List 13.1853 [*www.linguistlist.org/ issues/13/131853.html*. Jan. 28, 2003].

Works Cited

———. 2000. *Random House Webster's College Dictionary*. New York: Random House.

———. 2001. *Merriam Webster's Collegiate Dictionary*. Springfield, Mass.: Merriam-Webster, Inc.

Alford, H. 1864. *A Plea for the Queen's English*. New York: Routledge.

Baldwin, T. W. 1944. *William Shakespere's Small Latine & Lesse Greeke*. 2 vols. Urbana: University of Illinois Press.

Balme, M., and J. Morwood. 1987. *Oxford Latin Course*. Oxford: Oxford University Press.

Barrow, T. 1955. *The Sanskrit Language*. London: Faber and Faber.

Bobbitt, F. 1924. *How to Make a Curriculum*. New York: Houghton Mifflin.

Braddock, R., R. Lloyd-Jones, and L. Schoer. 1963. *Research in Written Composition*. Champaign, Ill. National Council of Teachers of English.

Brod, R. 1975. "Foreign Language Enrollments in U.S. Colleges—Fall 1974." *ADFL Bulletin* 7.2 (November): 37–44.

Brod, R., and E. B. Welles. 1998. "Foreign Language Enrollments in United States Institutions of Higher Education, Fall 1998." *ADFL Bulletin* 31.2 (winter 2000): 22–29.

Brooks, C. 1947. *The Well-Wrought Urn: Studies in the Structure of Poetry*. New York: Reynal and Hitchcock.

Bursill-Hall, G. L. 1971. *Speculative Grammars of the Middle Ages*. Paris: Mouton.

Caxton, W. 1910. "Prologue to Vergil's Eneydos (1490)." In *Prefaces and Prologues to Famous Books, Harvard Classics*. Edited by C. W. Eliot. New York: P. F. Collier & Son: 25–28.

Chomsky, N. 1957. *Syntactic Structures*. Paris: Mouton.

———. 1985. *Knowledge of Language: Its Nature, Origin, and Use*. New York: Praeger.

Cremin, L. A. 1961. *The Transformation of the School: Progressive Education in American Education 1876–1957*. New York: Vintage Books.

d'Andeli, H. 1914. "The Battle of the Seven Arts." In *Memoirs of the University of California, IV.1*, edited and translated from the French by L. J.Paetow. Berkeley: University of California Press.

Davis, F. 1984. "A Defense of Grammar," *English Education* 16.3 (October): 162–65.

Dewey, J. 1916. *Democracy and Education: An Introduction to the Philosophy of Education*. New York: Macmillan.

Dod, B. G. 1982. "Aristotle latinus." In *Cambridge History of Later Medieval Philosophy*. Cambridge: Cambridge University Press.

Elbow, P. 1981. *Writing With Power: Techniques for Mastering the Writing Process*. New York: Oxford University Press.

Elley, W. B., I. H. Barham, H. Lamb, and M. Wyllie. 1975/1976. "The Role of Grammar in a Secondary School English Curriculum." *New Zealand Journal of Educational Studies* 10 (May): 26–42. Reprinted in *Research in the Teaching of English* ("The Official Bulletin of National Council of Teachers of English") 10.1 (spring 1976): 5–21.

Erasmus, D. 1979. *The Praise of Folly. Translated with an introduction and commentary by Clarence H. Miller*. New Haven, Conn.: Yale University Press.

Fowler, H. W. 1926. *A Dictionary of Modern English Usage*. Oxford: Clarendon.

Fries, C. 1925. "The Periphrastic Future with Shall and Will in Modern English." *PMLA* XL: 963–1024.

Fries, C. 1952. *The Structure of English: An Introduction to the Construction of English Sentences*. New York: Harcourt Brace.

Gibb, H. 1963. *Arabic Literature: An Introduction*. Oxford: Clarendon.

Haskins, C. H. 1929. *Studies in Mediaeval Culture*. Oxford: Clarendon.

Hillocks, G., Jr. 1986. *Research on Written Composition: New Directions for Teaching*. Urbana, Ill: Clearinghouse on Reading and Communication Skills, National Institute for Education.

Hillocks, G., Jr., and M. W. Smith. 1991. "Grammar and Usage." In *Handbook of Research on Teaching the English Language Arts*, edited by J. Flood. New York: Macmillan.

Hirsch, E. D., Jr. 1987. *Cultural Literacy: What Every American Needs to Know*. Boston: Houghton Mifflin.

Hook, J. N. 1975. *History of the English Language*. New York: Ronald Press.

Huddleston, R. D., and G. K. Pullum. 2002. *The Cambridge Grammar of the English Language*. Cambridge: Cambridge University Press.

———. 2003. "Of Grammatophobia." *Chronicle of Higher Education*. Section 2, *Chronicle Review*, January 3, 2003: B20.

Hunt, R. 1985. "Reading as Writing: Meaning-making and Sentence Combining." In *Sentence Combining: A Rhetorical Perspective*, edited by D. A. Daiker, A. Kerek, and M. Morenberg, 159–74. Carbondale: Southern Illinois University Press.

John of Salisbury. 1955. *The Metalogicon*. Translated from the Latin by D. D. McGarry. Berkeley: University of California Press.

Kilpatrick, W. 1951. *Philosophy of Education*. New York: Macmillan.

Kirk, G. S. 1985. *The Iliad: A Commentary*. Cambridge: Cambridge University Press.

Kolln, M. 1982. *Understanding English Grammar*, 1st ed. New York: Macmillan.

———. 2001. "The Changing Status of Grammar," *Syntax in the Schools* 17.2 (autumn): 5–6.

———. 2003. *Rhetorical Grammar: Grammatical Choices, Rhetorical Effects*, 4th ed. New York: Longman.

Kolln, M., and R. Funk. 2002. *Understanding English Grammar*, 6th ed. New York: Longman.

LaFleur, R. A. 1992. "Classical Language Enrollments in the Colleges and Schools," *The Classical Outlook* 69: 120–122.

Latacz, J. 1996. *Homer, His Art and His World*. Ann Arbor: University of Michigan Press.

Lester, M. 1990. *Grammar and Usage in the Classroom*. New York: Macmillan.

Lily, W. 1544. *An Introduction of the Eyght Partes of Speche, and the Construction of the Same*. Londini: In officina Thomae Bertheleti. Microfilm. Ann Arbor, Mich.: University Microfilms International, 1985. (Early English books, 1475–1640; 1835:25)

———. 1673. *A Short Introduction of Grammar Generally to Be Used*. Oxford: At the Theatre. Microfilm. Ann Arbor, Mich.: University Microfilms International, 1985. (Early English Books, 1641–1700; 1529:19)

Lily, W., and J. Colet. 1970. *A Short Introduction of Grammar (1549)*. Menston, England: Scolar Press.

Lowth, R. 1967. *A Short Introduction to English Grammar (1762)*. Menston, England: Scolar Press.

Macauley, W. J. 1947. "The Difficulty of Grammar." *British Journal of Educational Psychology* 17: 153–162.

McIntosh, J. 2000. *Nimble Believing: Dickinson and the Unknown*. Ann Arbor: University of Michigan Press.

McNeill, W. H. 1974. *The Shape of European History*. Oxford: Oxford University Press.

Morenberg, M. 1991. *Doing Grammar*. New York: Oxford University Press.

Moynihan, D. P. 1993. "Defining Deviancy Down: How We've Become Accustomed to Alarming Levels of Crime and Destructive Behavior." *The American Scholar* (winter): 17–30.

Murray, C. and R. J. Herrnstein. 1992. "What's Really Behind the SAT-Score Decline?" *Public Interest* (winter): 32–56.

Murray. L. 1968. *English Grammar* (1795). Menston, England: Scolar Press.

Norton, A. O. 1909. *Readings in the History of Education: Medieval Universities*. Boston: Harvard University Press.

Padley, G. A. 1976. *Grammatical Theory in Western Europe, 1500–1700: The Latin Tradition*. Cambridge: Cambridge University Press.

———. 1985. *Grammatical Theory in Western Europe, 1500–1700: Trends in Vernacular Grammar*. Cambridge: Cambridge University Press.

Phillips, M. 1996. *All Must Have Prizes*. London: Little, Brown.

Piltz, A. 1981. *The World of Medieval Learning*. Translated from the Swedish by D. Jones. New York: Barnes & Noble.

Pinborg, J. 1982. "Speculative Grammar." In *Cambridge History of Later Medieval Philosophy*, edited by N. Kretzmann, A. Kenny, and J. Pinborg. Cambridge: Cambridge University Press: 254–270.

Pinker, S. 1994. *The Language Instinct: How the Mind Creates Language*. New York: William Morrow.

Powell, B. B. 1991. *Homer and the Origin of the Greek Alphabet*. Cambridge: Cambridge University Press.

Proctor, R. E. 1998. *Defining the Humanities: How Rediscovering a Tradition Can Improve Our Schools*. Bloomington: Indiana University Press.

Ravitch, D. 2000. *Left Back: A Century of Failed School Reforms*. New York: Simon and Schuster.

Rebhorn, W. A. 2000. *Renaissance Debates on Rhetoric*. Ithaca, N.Y.: Cornell University Press.

Reed, A., and B. Kellogg. 1875. *Graded Lessons in English*. New York: Clark and Maynard.

———. 1987. *Higher Lessons in English (1886)*. Ann Arbor: Scholars' Facsimiles and Reprints.

Robb, K. 1994. *Literacy and Paideia in Ancient Greece*. Oxford: Oxford University Press.

Sandys, J. 1905. *Harvard Lectures on the Revival of Learning*. Boston: Harvard University Press.

Schneider, J., and S. von der Emde. 2000. "Brave New (Virtual) World: Transforming Language Learning into Cultural Studies Through Online Learning Environments (MOO's)."*ADFL Bulletin* 31.2 (fall): 18–26.

Schulz, R. 2002. "Changing Perspectives in Foreign Language Education: Where Do We Come from? Where Are We Going? *Foreign Language Annals 35.3* (May, June): 285–91.

Searle, J. 1996 "Literary Theory and Its Discontents." In *Beyond Poststructuralism: The Speculations of Theory and the Experience of Reading*, edited by W. V. Harris, 101–36. University Park: Pennsylvania State University Press.

Small, R. C., Jr., and Members of NCTE's Standing Committee on Teacher Preparation and Certification. 1996. *Guidelines for the Preparation of Teachers of English Language Arts*. Urbana, Ill.: National Council of Teachers of English.

Smart, P. R. 1969. *Let's Learn English in the 70's*. Wellington, New Zealand: A. H. and A. W. Reed.

Sum, A., I. Kirsch, and R. Taggart. 2002. "The Twin Challenges of Mediocrity and Inequality: Literacy in the U.S. from an International Perspective." Princeton, N.J.: Policy Information Center, Educational Testing Service.

Tucker, H. 2000. "The Place of the Personal: The Changing Face of Foreign Language Literature in a Standards Based Curriculum," *ADFL Bulletin* 31.2 (winter): 53–58.

Visser, F. T. 1963–73. *An Historical Syntax of the English Language*. Leiden: Brill.

Wallace, D. F. 2001. "Tense Present: Democracy, English, and the Wars over Usage," *Harper's* (April): 39–58.

Washburne, C.W. and S.P. Marland. 1963. *Winnetka: The History and Significance of an Educational Experiment*. Englewood Cliffs, N.J.: Prentice Hall.

Watson, F. 1968. *The Old Grammar Schools*. London: Franks Cass.

Weaver, C. 1996. *Teaching Grammar in Context*. Portsmouth N.H.: Boynton/Cook.

Wheelock, F.M. 1956. *Latin: An Introductory Course Based on Ancient Authors*. New York: Barnes & Noble.

Index